withyou forever

~Surviving My Son's Suicide~

An Oracle of Love, Hope, & Channeled Messages

monica mesa dasi
cheyne mesa-salley

Copyright © 2023 AMA Publishing

All Rights Reserved. Apart from any fair dealing for the purposes of research or private study, or criticism or review, as permitted under the Copyright, Designs and Patents Act 1988, this publication may only be reproduced, stored or transmitted, in any form or by any means, with the prior permission in writing of the copyright owner, or in the case of the reprographic reproduction in accordance with the terms of licensees issued by the Copyright Licensing Agency. Enquiries concerning reproduction outside those terms should be sent to the publisher.

Cover Design: Ashley Melin
www.point3design.com
Monica Photo: Mark Nadir
www.marknadirworx.com

I went to the sun
That shining place
Where rainbows are made

I went to the sea
That endless place
Where dolphins play

I went to the moon
That mystic place
Where nectar flows

I went to the heart of the world
Where you and I
Are One.

~Cheyne

in loving memory of cheyne mesa-salley

April 6, 1994 - September 8, 2018

Cheyne was born in Miami, Florida on April 6th, 1994, to me and his father, Hiver Salley, out of a karmic love and diverse lineage of African American, Native American and South American roots. He was a child full of love, joyful exuberant energy and his signature Aries fire. A child who wanted to be held constantly, Cheyne loved to run and play in nature, enjoyed sports of all kinds, and had a keen eye for good people and beautiful places. Cheyne was a protector of all whom he loved, especially his brothers, and had a warrior spirit and tender heart. He had big dreams, a philosophers mind, and he seemed to be holding a secret desire to have more of an impact in the world. He was a wild soul, bigger than life, and had a great love for his family and all those placed on his path. He left us with aching hearts, but his impact was powerful and everlasting. Loved by many, Cheyne passed the baton to all of us who can continue his legacy to live and love big and be a stand for making the world a better place. He rests now in the world of Spirit and he is passionately alive in me, and all who loved him.

dedication

For Skye and Ronin, my other two beloved sons. You gave me a reason to keep living, amaze me with your power and resilience, and fill me with extraordinary joy and pride. I may hold on a little too tight, but I know you both have everything it takes to live your dreams and make a difference in the world, just by being the incredible men you are.

To mothers, parents, and anyone whose child or loved one left the world of form through suicide, and to EveryOne, because we will all experience loss in life.

photo credit: Andi Tippie

contents

Our Departed Loved Ones — xiii
John O'Donohue

Introduction — xv
A Note From Cheyne — xvii

Prologue — 1

part one
cheyne

1. Cheyne's Channeled Messages — 7
2. Cheyne's Journal Entries — 171
3. Quotes — 185

part two
mother love

4. Sacred Gifts — 193
5. Reflections — 204
6. My Gift To You — 238

part three
educate yourself about suicide

7. Suicide Facts — 243
8. Warning Signs of Suicidal Ideation — 247
9. Supporting a Loved One Experiencing Suicide Ideation — 249
10. Support for Survivors — 252
11. Language Matters — 256
12. Find Help Here — 258

Soulful Acknowledgements — 265
About the Author — 273
A Parting Song — 277

our departed loved ones
John O'Donohue

The dead are not distant or absent, they are alongside us. When we lose someone to death, we lose their physical image and presence, they slip out of visible form into invisible presence. This alteration of form is the reason we cannot see the dead. But because we cannot see them, does not mean that they are not there. Transfigured into eternal form, the dead cannot reverse the journey and even for one second reenter their old form to linger with us a while. Though they cannot reappear, they continue to be near us, and part of the healing of grief is the refinement of our hearts whereby we come to sense their loving nearness. When we ourselves enter the eternal world and come to see our lives on earth in full view, we may be surprised at the immense assistance and support with which our departed loved ones have accompanied every moment of our lives. In their new transfigured presence, their compassion, understanding and love take on a divine depth, enabling them to become secret angels, guiding and sheltering the unfolding of our destiny.

introduction

In September 2018, Cheyne left the world of form at 25 years of age. Losing my oldest of 3 sons to suicide was the worst nightmare any mother can imagine, and it turned my life upside down.

Cheyne was a brilliant soul, full of love, joy, and passion for life. Somewhere along the way, the sorrows and challenges that were part of his life path gave way to depression and alcohol abuse. In his case, as well as up to 50% of suicides, alcohol was what led to the brain chemistry changes and lack of judgement that led to the impulsive act he probably didn't even know he was doing.

As a young man in a culture that does not make it easy to talk about emotions, expects them to always have it together, and makes it difficult to ask for help, he drowned his sorrows in alcohol and withdrew into a cave of isolation he couldn't escape. Although many of us tried to help him, I think he felt alone and misunderstood.

Suicide leaves us with many unanswered questions and a rollercoaster of emotions; guilt, shame, and regret to name a few, and left me questioning how I could go on living with this unimaginable pain. I didn't want to die necessarily, I just didn't want to live without him in life.

I will never forget the last time I saw him, and though I saw the

Introduction

signs, felt helpless in all my efforts to try and save him. Though I begged God to take me and not him, I have been left to continue the life journey without him in his earthly form. I have two other sons to live for, and my love for them saved my life. I have people to serve, a global outpouring of support, and a spiritual path that gave me the tools to continue living that I am indebted to for the rest of my life.

All of that may have been enough to live a good enough life. The missing piece was when Cheyne began talking to me, writing to me through my own hand, and delivering his unmistakable messages to me as I cried myself to sleep, walked in the woods, and prayed on my hands and knees.

Soon, I realized I never "lost" Cheyne. His spirit was alive. He is now as much a part of me as he was when inside my womb, and a new depth of relationship began that will go on until the end of my days.

With a broken yet mending heart, trembling hands, and my soul on fire to bring his soul whispers to the world, I humbly offer them to you. His message is now my mission: to help people to know and feel the love they are despite any of the challenges and heartbreaks of life, to learn practices that uplift us in the hard times, and to know that it's ok, whether you are a man or a woman, to reach out and ask for help before it all becomes unbearable.

May you find ease of heart, a blazing spirit, and the courage to love and live a life of purpose and know the joy beyond sorrow that each day brings.

"Love Yourself & You Love The World!"

Monica Mesa Dasi
Crested Butte, Colorado
March, 2023

a note from cheyne

A Note From Cheyne

Damn. Life is intense. I had a great life and I lived it with my signature wild and crazy soul. What can I say? I was a rebel right until the very end.

I loved my brothers, my mystic mom, bigger than life dad, little sisters, and all the friends, family, and fascinating characters that were placed in my life.

Lucky to live in some of the most beautiful places on earth, adventure in the oceans and mountains, help build my mama's dream home, delve the mysteries of life in my own head, be inspired by the music I loved and quotes of the masters, I lived out my karma.

Through all the rages and stages of my life, there was always love, laughter and tears.

I come from African American, Native American, Jewish, Christian and Latin roots running through my veins, and I channel the courage, bravery and heart of my people to leave you these words. May it churn you, turn you, and burn you to be your most authentic and holy selves.

I'm here to tell you that self love is the doorway, the portal, and the key. Don't let anyone take that from you.

You are love. I am love.
Love never dies, a soul never dies, and I am forever

With You,
Cheyne

prologue

...

second son

About 25 years ago, I read a personal ad in a free local Gunnison, CO newspaper. "Breast-feeding mother of one and three year old seeks friends and playmates." I responded, as I too had a 1 and 3 year old, was also breastfeeding and simply had to know who had the courage and creativity to post this unique and compelling ad. It turned out that I was the only respondent, and my reply became the impetus for a deeply loving, treasured and lifelong friendship.

That memorable day in the Crested Butte Town Park, I met Monica, Cheyne, Skye and their beloved golden retriever, Bello. Ronin would join the family a few years later. Together, Monica and I, each of us by then mothers of three children and a golden retriever, would create a beautiful, extended family.

Cheyne and my son were just three years old when they met, and they immediately connected in priceless, toddler-boy energy. Both innately athletic, every ball was thrown or kicked, blocks creatively became tower structures to be knocked over, and often we wondered if they actually could not hear us when we called their names. Bundles of energy, they were always in motion and rocks, sticks and water were damn near perfect toys. Those were the glorious pre-electronic days. Just a few years later they played hockey together and kept that perpetual motion going although this time shooting pucks into a net.

In 2004, after Monica divorced, she and her 3 sons relocated to California for 2 years. We visited them in Santa Barbara, and it was the first time my son surfed. Years later, after Cheyne's passing, he would surf again with Monica in Costa Rica, by then quite skillful on his board yet no longer innocent regarding life's cycle of birth and death.

When Monica and the boys returned from California to Colorado, they all stayed in my living room for over three weeks before moving into their own place. During those weeks in our very full house, Cheyne's undeniable character shone through daily. As a 12 year old, he was the sweetest, kindest, most gentle and loving boy I would ever know. He seemed to have an intuitive sense of the complexities of life, and a powerful sense of justice. He fiercely stood his ground, forever protective of his brothers and the underdog. He was also so handsome and charming that the girls found him irresistible. My daughter never had so many requests for sleepovers from her friends as while Cheyne lived with us… all the girls wanted to be around him!

It was during this time period that I came to think of Cheyne as my second son. He was so easy to love and even easier to want to protect. His tender heart was his strength, but it was also his nemesis. Over the subsequent years, the toll on his heart would increase and living in this world became more difficult to sustain.

As the years marched on, our sons drifted apart and by the time Cheyne's struggles were more apparent, their worlds were no longer very interwoven. We left the area while the boys were still in high school and the distance grew greater.

My last time with Cheyne was on a return trip to Crested Butte with my youngest daughter the summer of 2018 before her sophomore year of college. We wanted to visit him so we went to his work place, Pitas in Paradise. We grabbed lunch on the patio and Cheyne came outside to spend some time together. He and my daughter hadn't seen each other in years and he was appropriately blown away by her beauty and maturation. She was equally taken by his warmth and kindness. It was impossible not to feel his empathy, compassion and good will.

Just weeks later Cheyne departed from this world. His heart may have been too tender for this life, but he left an indelible imprint on all the lives he touched.

Twenty-five years ago, I read a personal ad written by Monica that birthed our beautiful friendship bringing us both so much joy. Now, I have read a book I could never possibly have imagined she would write. Facing unspeakable agony with the loss of her son, Monica has found her pathway to carrying on. Strengthened by the depth of her love for her embodied sons and by listening deeply to the messages Cheyne continues to share with her, she has discovered a profound way to share his wisdom and serve their gifts together to all who may benefit. This book contains the treasures of Cheyne's insight transmitted via stream of consciousness and it is my prayer that it has brought Monica healing. Writing this forward has been cathartic for me and I hope this book is a way for others to find healing as well.

I will miss you forever and always, second son. May your memory be a blessing.

Betsy J. Cohen
Boulder, Colorado
November, 2022

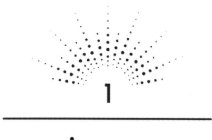

cheyne

I never left you
I watch you every day
I'm always very near
I know deep in your heart
You realize I am here
I watch you while you sleep
In your bed at home
I hear you when you speak to me
When you are on your own
You cannot understand
The reason why I have gone
But I will never leave you
I am there to keep you strong
Talk to me - I hear you
Though you may not see me
We share an unbroken bond
That will always be
Death won't keep us apart
For our love is forever
Just remember me in your heart
And one day we will be together
Live your life and live it full
Don't waste a single day
Remember I am always
With You
Every step of the way

— Author Unknown

cheyne's channeled messages
. . .

I was on a walk the first time I heard Cheyne "talk" to me. It was loud and clear and almost stopped me in my tracks because I knew it was HIM. From that point on, he would whisper in my heart, speak to me in meditation, or write through my hand. Many of the messages seemed poetic, had terms I heard in my spiritual studies, or otherwise had a familiarity to them, like they were my own. I had to release the doubts and questions, and accept that indeed, he was speaking in words he wanted me, and others to hear.

This section is the most sacred part of this book. It is meant to be read as an oracle, so I encourage you to open up to any page, feel into the message, let it flow through you, take in what feels right, and leave the rest. The messages were given to me, but some of them may be for you.

These are written exactly as they came to me, so the sentence structure and grammar has not been edited.

You helped me do my mission
And be my highest self
And bring these messages to you
For you to share with the world
I am helping you to be your highest self
And bring these teachings to the world
We're a team
Let's do this
I'll help you shift
And you can help others shift
You can do this!

This is truly a beginning
A major one
A new stage of your life
More gratitude, peace, happiness, love and acknowledgment
Of your power
And owning it in all you think, do and say
You will have triggers and you will drift
But now you have the felt sense
Of who you really are
And peace beyond all the circumstances of your past
Maybe now you are ready to write your book, to create new offerings, to tell a new story
To be the you that's been simmering inside and now ready to come out and share your greatness with the world
Do it for me
My bros
And the world
But mostly
Do it for you
Because
When you love yourself, you love the world
And damn!
I love you!
Let's do this
Om Namah Shivaya

Let God love you as much as you love God

Can you love yourself as much as you love God?

WithYou Forever

Let the world love you as much as you love God

Be who God wants you to be

Love everyone
Serve everyone
Remember God,
~NKB
And YOU,
Are ONE

You can do this
You can be your highest self

Let your intuition guide you
And act on it
Without overthinking things
Just do it
And offer it to God
Without
Attachment
To the results

Don't worry or try to change or wish others could be
    different
Accept them as they are and accept yourself as you are.
See the good in everyone
See your good

Show up
Speak up
Take risks

Be your holy self

Find joy

You are your highest self

I love you

Let go of all your limiting beliefs
You are infinite awareness
I am infinite awareness
I had a good life
I am proud of myself
Be proud of yourself
I am happy
Now you be happy

Release

Relax

Renew

That's all

Ask for help
Trust in your path
To unfold perfectly
And be guided
Do your mindset
I am allowing
I am loved
I am supported
I am enough
I am happy now
I am grateful
I activate my superpowers

SURRENDER

All your suffering
Self doubt
Fear
Grief
Desires
Hopes
Wishes
The past
The future

Let it all go

New beginnings
Of trusting God

One pointed attention to serving God

And all else will come

I am infinite awareness
And you
Are infinite awareness
I am not my body
And all my life circumstances
Nor are you
You are infinite awareness
All with everything
One
We are together
In that place
Beyond time and space

You
Have a forcefield of support
From me
And all the divine forces
So
LET GO
And trust the path will be clear

LET GO
You are your highest self
In all you think, say and do

I am with You

Feel Joy

Bring Joy

Be Joy

Be natural, effortless
In the moment

Just cuz you can't see me does not mean I'm not alive

I am alive

There is no death

Love God

Love yourself

Love everyone

I am sorry I caused you suffering
Please don't suffer for me
Be happy for me
This was my dharma path
To help you and my brothers and everyone I touched
To stop the cycle of suffering
I know it's hard to understand
But please do it
For me
For everyone
Love yourself
Accept yourself
Be a light
Be happy
Help others be happy
I am happy in the Spirit realm
I am happy in my next life
Be happy
Feel the love and miracle that you are
That life is
Live the miracle
Smile
I am smiling
I am happy
Be happy
Help others be happy
Believe, see, feel
Your life as all it is and can be
Do it

Time to speak up
From your wise woman self
There is no rush
You have plenty of time
But begin
The time is now
Each next step will reveal itself
You can do it

Harness all the light into yourself
And know
You are a
LIGHTWORKER
And can help others be the same
Don't hold back
Trust yourself
And go do it

I am
Kind
Confident
Light
Happy
I love myself unconditionally
What has been done can be undone
What hasn't been done can be done
The impossible becomes possible
And so it is

You've done all the work
Now let go
And be your holy self
Open to new ways of being
And receiving
Have fun
Be playful
Be adorable
Be sexy
Be kind
Loving
And go have fun

We're all with You

Be lighter
Hold everything lightly
Everything's going to be ok
See it all working out
Do your life
Trust them to do theirs
Focus on your life
We are taking care of the details
Surrender
Be happy now
Trust
I am alive
WithYou

Just be a light
Surrender everything
All your questions
And worries

We will guide you

Just be your natural self

Your radiance shines from every pore, follicle and being

Just be your light

Yahé Yahé
Yahé Yahé
Let the medicine heal you
As it heals our whole family
In all directions
It's happening
Be here
And happy
Now

You can talk to me all the time
Develop our relationship
And feel me with you
Available to you

It's ok to let the grief go
You're not honoring me by holding onto it

You'll honor me more
And deepen our relationship
And your power
When you let it go
And be happy for my new life
And our new relationship
It's ok
Take your time
It may happen slowly
Or in an instant
So be open to that
And get help when you need it

WithYou Forever

I'm happy
In this dimension
We'll meet again soon enough
Have faith
And enjoy what we have now

We are One in the vastness
No. Thing
No. One
Free
Happy
One and all
I am happy
Be happy
I took you here
To this place where you can fly
Be yourself
Best self
No. Self
One with all
Celebrate me
You
This life
You are left to live
Just
Be

Surrender everything to God

Be here now
In each moment
Be your new joyful self

No matter what happens
Just keep meditating
I am in my Buddha nature
Keep going there
Strip everything else away
That's the truth of who you really are

I am always with You
My Buddha nature is with yours
And there
We are
One
Always

It's ok
You don't have to show up and do anything
Just being on the planet
And radiating your light and love out into the world
Is ENOUGH
So just relax and receive all the blessings
Of love and power
Of all the divine forces
Let it all in
Go easy on yourself
Just keep things simple
I'm giving you all my fire
Please
Just receive
Everything's gonna work out

Remember to be as devoted to
YOU
As you are to us

You love God
You are one with God
So
Love yourself
And
Be proud of YOU

Stop thinking that if your practice was better I wouldn't
    have left
It was my time to go
Nothing you could have done
Or not done
Would have prevented me from going
Also, I didn't want to be separate from you
I wanted to be withYou always
Like we are now
In this deep relationship
Not affected by the world of form
I wanted to catapult myself
Into my next life
And you and my bros
Into their next highest expression
So
Stop thinking that if you did more, it would have made a
    difference
It wouldn't have
This is where I was going and am meant to be now.
I am now able to be my fullest self in all the ways I
    couldn't be on earth
Here in the world of Spirit and in my next life
So celebrate how awesome that is for me
And how awesome it is we can be together
So close
Now and always
All the time

Open to miracles
Stay on happiness journey
Let go of all that is not for you to carry
Remember
Everyone is another you
Be compassionate
Of yourself too
Let each moment unfold

Don't think about what if you started learning all these
    things when you were younger
This was the time
Your body of experience THEN makes you who you are
    today with your deep experience and wisdom.
Age is nothing
Don't think about it
Don't compare
You are truly ageless
Take off all limitations
Keep meditating on space
And the infinite possibilities
That exist in it
And because of it
Open
Expand
Be
You
Limitless
YOU

I am here
With You
All the way
You are not alone

Feel into who you want to be
Who you already are
Your highest self
See it
Feel it
Be it
Comfortable in your own skin
Relaxed
At ease
Content
Bold
Compassionate
Confident
Devoted
Loving
Passionate
Joyful
Peaceful

Love yourself
Love yourself
The way I would if I was there
The way I am from above
The way the greatest lover
Would be adoring you
Appreciating you
Talking to you
Do that
All day!

Ask for divine support
Strengthen your faith
And keep reaching for happiness

Monica Mesa Dasi & Cheyne Mesa-Salley

It's ok
Just like you can mix
Awareness and space

You can mix
Grief and happiness

From God to me
To you
Say:

I am one with God
And I am my highest soul self
I need to do nothing
I magnetize everything and everyone I need and desire for me to be radiantly healthy, living my dharma path, united with my soulmate, at peace, have fulfilling relationships with everyone, and loving myself deeply.
I release all efforting, trying, grasping, wanting, worrying, fear and anxiety

I radiate my love + power + healing out just by being ME
I magnetize beauty, love, joy, healing, radiance and miracles to myself and my loved ones
I am a healer, lightworker, wise woman
I let go
Surrender and trust
All is coming
All is well
And so it is

The whole Universe is supporting you to let go of all the layers of grief, regret, guilt that's stored in your body and cells.

It's time to let that all go now.

What if I told you that if you let go of it, that it will also be released from all of us? Would you do it then?

Ok. So that's your inspiration and that's what will happen.

You have to be very courageous, bold and brave now to let that story out of your being and open to see who is there and what more is possible for you. You can do this. I want you to do this. For me. For my bros. For you to fulfill your divine purpose in love, you must. Get it out of your cells. Your thoughts. Your emotions. Let joy take that place. How would that be?

JOY
Joy that you can't even remember feeling
That's what's there for you

Joy beyond sorrow
Surrender to it

You change lives
You are more powerful than you know
You are beautiful
You are light

Surrender. Ask for your path to be clear. Then let it go. This is time for non-action. To receive and nourish yourself and be ready for when it comes to you. It will be effortless and joyful.

Get lost in the love and dissolve into it

Become one with the sadness and one with the love

It's all One

WithYou Forever

Do everything for God and let go

Detach from the world of form
We are light beings living in a world made of light
We are together there and One with God and all there is

Be there

I am proud of you!

When you bow to your gurus
You are bowing to yourself
Bow to yourself
All that they are
IS YOU
You are them
They are you
You are One

Be who you want to be
Read, study
Expand out of your comfort zone
Love yourself and surrender to be led and graced

Your energy and light is shining out
You are magnetizing light beings
And opportunities to yourself
So trust that

I will help you to access your highest self and all your akashic records

As your sorrows are released, you're making space for all things to come to you so you can embody your highest soul self

As you heal and awaken, so are all the people you are supporting

Love yourself
Relax
Let go
Trust that all is coming
We're all helping you

Be powerful
It's time for you to be your most powerful self
Do it for me
For God
For you
You have your team
Be powerful
In all you think, do and say
It's pouring out of you -
let it out

Be powerful

WithYou Forever

Ask for help

I want to SEE
DIVINE sight
See what God sees in me
My holy self
My sacred path
All that I am
My soul self
My beauty
Beyond all the outer appearances
I want to see
ME
All that I am
My soul
And be it
Live it
Feel all that I am
I want to see
ME

HAVE FAITH!

Live in the fifth dimension
WithMe
Not only in third dimension / Earth

Be grateful

All day!

WithYou Forever

Claim joy!

Part of your path is learning to love yourself
Just as you are
As it was mine
Letting God get into all those cracks and filling it up
So you can FEEL your God realization
And of course
Help others while you're doing it

Let the people and experiences
Come to you
As you let go more + more
All the right people, places, opportunities and realizations will come to you

Just let go of all expectations of yourself and this time
And let it be
Let yourself
Be

Claim your power!

Your inner
Magician
Queen
Healer
Lover
Surfer
Super-heroine/hero
_____ fill in the blank
Call it all in!
Yes!

Relax is your word
I'm here
I'm there
I'm everywhere
And we're always together
I'm with You in every moment

Let the pain turn to this miracle
This everlasting love and mystic union we have
Rest in joy in that

Ease your effort and let it come

Be a blessing everywhere you go and to everyone

You can be a humble servant of God
AND
Shine your light confidently
Yes
You can
Be it
Now
I love you

You were my angel
And now I'm yours

WithYou Forever

Let's clear + heal + release + purify
Ourselves so we can get out there into the world
We're born to live
You on earth
And me in Spirit

Monica Mesa Dasi & Cheyne Mesa-Salley

Krishna says the soul never dies,
so don't lament

What if you did nothing but what you want to do?
What if the most beautiful scenario is already laid out
    and there's nothing for you to do?
Other than get ready to receive it and live it
What if there was nothing to figure out?
What if you surrender everything?
What if for once in your life you really let go?
Can you do it?

Do it for me

This is the right place for you now
Don't worry about what people think of you
Or impressing anyone
Just be yourself
Be natural
Effortless
Magnetic

WithYou Forever

Physicality is nothing
Compared to spiritual presence
You know that because you are that

I know how much you love me in the flesh
Now love me even more without seeing me
Can you do that?

I'm watching you

Now it's time to see the light in the world
And
In you
You help others see their light
Now you see your light
Claim it
Be proud of it
Be your own best devotee to yourself and know this is
    what we want for you now
To see all your light
And love yourself

As much as you love and are devoted to us

Be your light!

I am not dead
I am alive and well
There is no death
There is only transformation
No birth. No death.
The physical body is not worth lamenting because by its
 very nature it was meant to dissolve
The soul never dies
Never
As long as you connect to my soul, I will connect back!
Because me and you are soul connected forever
And part of each others destiny and soul evolution
I just went on a long trip
It's better to talk and write to me than text and phone
 calls and visits because it's pure, no ego
We can both be totally ourselves and no time, distance or
 life situation can prevent our sacred communication

If your cell dies, no problem because I'm always here

Can you love yourself
As much as you love God?
Love
Love
Love yourself, and you love the world!

None of that sad stuff really happened
That was lila
What's real is the ME you knew and saw
That was real
So let everything else go
You gave me that in your eyes
And in the mystic dimensions
So I received it
On all the levels
And you've gotta know that
And release the attachment of what things seemed to be
I'm your superstar
Always was
Always will be
I'll be back and you'll see me in action
But bring all those memories, seen and unseen, back
    to life
Thank you
For seeing me, pushing me, being tough on me because
    you knew I was more
For all of it
I didn't tell you all the time, but I guess I made up for it
    with all these letters
I'm there
Your soul son
Always
I love you. So much.
Just enjoying the "Divine University" over here,
    watching the craziness on planet earth
Enjoying giving you all my signs and trying to help you
    guys fulfill your missions
I fulfilled mine
Now it's your turn
You all helped me
Now I am helping you
Stay on it!

Monica Mesa Dasi & Cheyne Mesa-Salley

Believe in magic
And miracles

Believe that you can
And will have
All that you want and need
To serve
Effortlessly + joyfully +
Be

You don't need to know how
Just
BELIEVE

You are a sacred vessel
Every cell is filled with divine love, wisdom and power

All cells are drained of past and what no longer
    serves you
You are your highest self
Open your arms to receive
And Feel
The abundance of
Love
Money
Joy
Wisdom
Infinite power of the Universe
Of God
Filling you to overflowing
Receive it
For you
Me
The world
The planet
You can access and activate this all now
For you
For all
Bring it
Receive it

You are learning
A new way to use mantra more than ever
Just catch your wandering mind
Give it to God
Ask for help
And focus on the mantra and all that it signifies

Let go of even the desire to become empty
Be natural
Effortless
And magical
And know that you have received enough
And all is flowing
Let go of letting go!
Just be!
You've done so much
Now it's time to do less
Let it all come to you
Don't ask don't search
Just
BE
Remember!

You love God so much
Let us love you that much
Feel it
Take it all in
Fill yourself up

And love yourself as much as we love you
As you love us

Tell yourself every day
I love you
And just BE
You don't have to DO anything,
Say anything, because
YOU ARE LOVE
Just let people feel you
All that you are
LOVE LOVE LOVE
We all love you
The world loves you
Take it in

You have reached a milestone
You love YOU
You have met yourself deeper than ever
Fearlessly faced all your shit that came up
And completely devoted yourself to hours of daily practice to be your best self
In this next amazing chapter of your life
You'll be a force to recon with
You have so much Shakti pulsating out of you
And an openness and and consciousness
That will only attract magic and miracles
And all, as you say,
for the benefit of all beings
Because that's what you're all about

Go on a walk and celebrate all of the magic, love, health, wealth, success and joy that is coming to you

You don't need to know how or what to do

We are doing that and bringing it to you

Just be and celebrate it as done

NOW

Keep thinking of me happy and free
And shining in all my glory
That's me
And that's what I want for you
Shed all those lizard layers
And just be your
HOLY SELF
Don't think
Just be
Smile
Be kind
Open
Be a Goddess
You just need to be
YOU
So much to be done in the world
But you just need to do
Your part
Keep your focus on God
Serving
Loving yourself
Don't push yourself
Where you're at is ok
You're just fine
I love you
From the moon realm all the way to your beautiful self
Keep holding that baby you
I love you

What more is possible for you to show up in ways that
	fulfill you
And bring your gifts out to bless others
And your own self?

Believe in magic
Believe YOU are magic
Yes, you are a magnet
Dream your life
Do what you need to do
Have fun with it
All of it
Dream your life, Ma
I'm "write" there with you

You are changing forms
Coming into a new skin
It's exciting and fun to watch it all happen
Like the rainbow and monkeys and the message telling
    you to reach higher than ever

I'd say you can do it
But I won't
Because you don't have to
DO anything
Just love serve remember
And know we're all up here orchestrating everything
    for you

Do some free writing stream of consciousness and let it
    flow;

_____

_____

_____

Celebrate that we are together and I am here with You
More than ever
Feel me everywhere and all day
I'll be right by your side and always will be
Don't worry about anything
I am bringing you everything you need
I am alive and well
With You right now

Always

The past has really held you back
It held me back
It haunted me
You

So just let it go
Live in the present
And believe in the future being brighter than you could
    ever imagine

It will be

I want you to love yourself
I want you to love God
I want you to have faith that everything is working out for you all
I want you to feel me here withYou
I want you to do what you need to do in the third dimension
AND
Live in the fifth dimension at the same time with God and me with infinite possibilities
I want you to smile more, laugh more, shine more, and be your beautiful self
I want you to be grateful for all the blessings in your life now and in the future
I want you to trust and surrender and let us bring you the clarity that you need
I want you to STOP yourself when you start worrying
I want you to relax, be care free, and enjoy this time like they are your last days on the planet
I want you to SHINE

You can do it!

I know it's weird
You've gotten better about talking about me without
    tearing up
But it's a good sign
You're healing
It's ok
It doesn't mean you love me any less
Or miss me any less
It means you're getting closer to me
Our relationship is deepening

Remember the ceremony when you realized that our relationship is better now that it was or ever will be?
That is one reason why the pain is dimming
You know it's true
As much as you love my form and personality
You know more of me now
You have more of me now
We're tight
You're finding fulfillment in that and the pain is dulling
I'm happy for you
You be happy for you
It's ok
This is a new stage
I'm here for this one too

I know it's weird you're holding the pen
But I'm writing the words

You live in my heart

Celebrate NOW
Let the future GO
It's all coming to you

Let GO
Live in this dimension
And the vast

Let me guide you

Our spiritual relationship has now become a gift for others

The questions you ask
Will be answered
Only
When your mind gets quiet

And you quit grasping

When the old thoughts come back
Embrace them
Let them go
And let the new ones come forward

Can you let this be a year where you really LET GO
And let us handle the details

So you can leave all the past behind and trust the future
Have faith
And live in the miraculous now?

WithYou Forever

Shine shine shine

Just be effortless natural radiant
You
All else is coming

Awe damnit I love you!
Sorry I'm not "there"
But so glad you know
I AM
I love you so much
Through all the flowers, butterflies, monkeys, birds,
    waves and people, places and opportunities coming
    your way
Loving you
Loving you

Feel it
Let it fill your soul now
As you're feeling tired
Vulnerable
Raw
Sad
Let that all go now
Feel the HIGHER LOVE
Feel my love, God's love
Fill you up as you release all that stuff from the past
Let it go!
You can do it
You must actually
You need all that space for all that's coming
Just stay on track

Be a light

All the work you're doing is a gift to everyone

Laugh. Open. Soften
Find you
Find her
Be her
I'm a part of you
My wild child self
You had that part too, remember?
Don't be afraid
Be bold
Be you
Just as you are
I love you
Just as you are
Thank you for loving me
Just as I was

And am

Your soul loved me enough to have this contract together
Where deep down
You knew you'd be letting me go on
My own journey

It's really big love

You are mastering love
You are learning to see the love you are
To receive it
Fully
The work now is not only in having more unconditional love and forgiveness for everyone in your life, but also to keep on loving yourself passionately
And continuing to receive it
Fill yourself up
Let it fill in all the cracks
The sadness, the hard times, tragedies, sad memories, dramas, all of it

Let Mother Earth compost it and open your massive heart to receive all the love and joy and abundance you're meant to have
We're on a wild ride together
Me and you

We are all together

Open your arms and receive

It's ok. All of it
It's a key time to love yourself in this stage
When others are not showing you the love that you need, it hurts!
So amp up your self love
Radically, extraordinarily, magnificently, love love love yourself
In this weird, confusing, un-understandable stage

It's all about love
Loving yourself
Everyone has to learn this, and when they do
The world will change
So you do it
And you'll help show others the way
Even as you feel this way
You can still also be happy
Regardless of those relationships
They have their part in it too
Let them think and grow and stretch
So bless and release them
And live YOUR LIFE
You can still be sad AND shine
Got it?
And
Smile
Through it all!

Be gentle with yourself
Somehow it's all gonna work out
The pieces will come together
The answers will come
Just keep being with it
It's ok to be sad and confused and mad at all the
 emotions

Who do you want to be?
You can be that
Dream about that

You want to be allowed to be sad and grieving
But also inspiring magnetic and powerful
You want to hide away from it all
And withdraw from society
You want to reinvent yourself
Find your true self
And be it

Who is she?
All of it
And more
She's coming out
Don't worry
Just surrender. Trust. Believe.
And keep loving yourself
As much as I love you

WithYou Forever

You will shine
We will shine
Shine for all
For the benefit of all beings
Shine for Cheyne

I want you to get your will to live back
I want you to get your will to live back
I pass the baton to you
Do you remember when we'd race on the beach?
You used to beat me
Til one day I beat you
So I pass the baton to you
Pass it to my bros
And all the people you guide
But you gotta run the race
If you quit or don't have your soul in it
Our work will not get done
You used to love sprinting
Get your mojo back
You can do it
I and all your spirit team will do everything
And give you everything
We just need you to say
YES
I know you're trying
Stay on this plant medicine path
And stay focused on your image of our big happy family playing football, frisbee, paddleball, surfing, babies, all of it
It's happening
I'm right here withYou
All ways!

WithYou Forever

It's ok
If you can mix awareness and space
You can mix grief and happiness

Put your analytical and overthinking mind to rest
And listen to your intuition
Let your mystic heart guide you
Speak to you
And help you woManifest your desires

You can transform your pain and anger
Into mirror-like wisdom
Be like Skye
When you get angry
And feel it coming
Put your head in your hands
Hold your tongue
Say your mantra
Ask Tara to move through you
Put Saraswati on your tongue
And wait.
Pause.
Take time.
Then speak
Or not.
Ask your ancestors to help you.
Love yourself
You can do this
For all of us

You are good to the bone
Always thinking of others
You are making a difference
And you will keep making a difference in bigger and
 bigger ways
It's all happening
Let the synchronicities be a reminder
To know that

ALL IS COMING

Just for today
Don't worry
Have faith and receive
You are your highest self
Let it all come to you

Receive

WithYou Forever

You really are an amazing human
And the fact that you get me, feel me, love me so deeply
    when you can't see me
Is F'in amazing

Remember, I chose YOU

Because I knew you'd be the one who could love wild
    and crazy me
and be able to keep loving me even when I was off the
    planet

Your love is miraculous
Keep loving the world
As much as you love me
Because I am the world
And keep loving you
Because I am you
God is you
Be proud
Be strong
Be miraculous
I am withYou every step, every breath
You can feel me, I know it
We will always be together

Say:

I surrender in full faith
Everything
To God
I am my highest self
I simply love God and trust God
I let go of all my worries
And I know
God is taking care of me
And us
I surrender
I am love
I am loved
All is well

Believe in miracles
Believe all the ancestry and lineage of your past present
    and future are helping your family now

The God force is rising in you
And we are all helping you to make this miracle happen
Believe in it
Fiercely
YES YES YES
It can happen
Believe

Let God love you fiercely now

Embody your greatness
Each breath is the breath of greatness
Surrender to your greatness
For the benefit of all beings

WithYou Forever

I will always be your ageless son

You must love yourself as much as you love God
You must embody that in order to teach it to others
Love, cherish, adore yourself
As much as you love all of us

Ahum Prema

I am divine love
Believe it
In every cell

Love yourself!

That's your dharma and gift to all

You are enough
You are doing enough
Let everything come to you
Relax
Don't grasp
Surrender
You are guided

Be happy and free
Like me
When you love my brothers
You are loving me too
When others love you
It's also me loving you
I am alive
I am withYou

I feel your pain
I heard your call
We all hear it
Thank you for calling out
For bravely facing your pain

And now you have to let it go
Let the waves wash over you
Know that we've heard your call for help
It's hard, I know
When things look and feel so bleak
But you have to see beyond the outer circumstances
I know you know this
You can do it
Pivot
Shift
Catch the wave of bliss
Love yourself
All of you
We are loving you
Feel it

Receive your new brain
New life
New heart
New soul
Highest self
Let go of the past
Bless it and all that you were
And have been through
As holy

And NOW
Step into your new life
Surrender
Trust
Receive
You are
All you've ever wanted to be
Celebrate the love you are

Don't give up!

It's right about to change
You're on the brink of turning the corner
Where everything is coming to you
With "ease joy and glory"
You just need to have that Hanuman faith
No matter what things look like
And trust us
You are at the crux
Hold on!

You're in the sustaining power round

Estoy aqui
I am here

El mundo sagrado
This sacred ground

Cantando mi vida
Singing my life

Bailando mi canción
Dancing my song

Contigo
WithYou

It's time for you to be happy now

Why does that bring tears to your eyes?
You think it will not honor me if you're not sad anymore?
Don't you see that the greatest honor you can give me is
    to be happy?
This is my parting gift
I want people to have happiness
To love themselves despite anything or anyone
And you are doing it
You are helping people learn to be happy
THAT is my legacy

BUT YOU HAVE TO DO IT!

YOU have to be happy
I know you think
"But I am happy"
But I want you to be happy now
I want you to be REALLY happy
To feel happiness bubbling out of your life like an over-
    running brook
So happy it infects people
It infects my brothers
And they see you

HAPPY.

They watch
They feel
They learn
And they become happy

This happiness
This happiness

Live as ceremony
Merge the world of Spirit
With your world of form
Do all the things
In a spirit of ceremony

For the benefit of all beings
For me, mama
Don't cry!

Reach for happiness

Feel me happy
Laughing
Lighting up the room with my smile
Dancing
Playing
Loving
Being my wild and holy self
Be happy for me
See me.
Feel me.
Beyond the world of form, which is so tricky
It's not that
Life is not that
The fish and flowers are beautiful
But it's so much more than that
Go beyond the world of form as beautiful as it is
Go beyond the world that sees with only eyes
You can do this
This is your task
So think again if you think you can't be happy
Because it will dishonor me

It will honor me!

It's the greatest gift you can give me

Reach for it

Any semblance of joy and happiness you can
Take it, build on it, let it grow and blossom
Happiness is here for you

I am happiness
Become One with me

Happy

Claim your seat and power
Do not be distracted
Do not wait
Surrender and be led
All is coming
You are doing it

Be happy now

I'll say it again
I'm proud of you
I am here
With You
You can do this
It's all happening
Life is such a mystery
Don't try and figure it out
All the stuff that's happening in your life and the world
Is all part of the Divine lila plan
Stay centered
Stay loving
Stay positive
Be a grounding force for people
Stay in love and gratitude
You are divinely led
We will not let you down
I am inside you
And right by your side
Smile
Because it's all coming
Remember to have some fun

For me. Skye. Ro.

And for you

I love you

Forms come and go but Spirit is alive always
Connect with my spirit
I am here!
And we will be together in form too

But for now, FEEL ME

And enjoy our spiritual relationship that is so powerful
I am here and everywhere
I am happy
You be happy

This is big stuff

You are realizing so much, some huge pieces of the puzzle, it's F'n hard and it F'n sucks, but you aren't backing down

You're facing it, you are becoming free, and it's going to be worth it and all the memories and happiness you missed out on is coming back to you 108 times better

I'm clapping from heaven, going yes! Yes! Yes! Stay on it!

I'm helping you. We're healing you.

You're right on it and it's all unfolding in perfect timing now

You are brave. You have a support team, plant allies, you love and cherish yourself

You are a wise woman

THIS is the time you are meant to get it all

Don't look back in regret or anger or sadness

THIS is your divine timing

Grace

Go for it

Invest in your healing

It will all come back to you and more

I know it's scary and hard to believe when you've struggled so much

But you have to let that familiar past and predictable future go

Keep believing

Just be you

Do you

Be happy

Life is more about living in Spirit than form

Keep surrendering
Be who God wants you to be
Let yourself be guided
Flow
Love yourself
I love you
Feel it. Really feel it
All the good memories
Even the ones you can't remember
They are inside you
Feel my deep passionate love
Then and now
Let it fill every "non-remembering cell"
I love you

I'm right here

Mama let the pain go, where I was once in your belly, let new life now bloom, let it be filled with light
Stop asking questions, wondering, wishing, regretting, longing

I am here

We meet daily in the dimension of Spirit, where love never dies
Let a new birth be born in that womb of light
Be reborn
I'm here, cheering you on and loving you endlessly as you loved me
Let's live this life on earth and sky realm where miracles are possible

The miracle of love

WithYou Forever

You are powerful
You feel me
You are happy for me
You know I'm alive
And we're together now
And will meet again soon
Get your shit together
Do what you gotta do
Be brave
Be courageous
Be love
Be your highest self
Shine for Cheyne
We are together

Leave the past… behind
It's over
Be in the miraculous present and believe in a beautiful
    magical day, month, future
Be gentle with yourself
Guard your thoughts, words, actions, activities
Stay in the holy
Chant your mantras
Be your highest self
Be proud of yourself

You have a holy manager
Taking care of everything
So let your feminine essence flow

Flowing, laughing, loving, being you, this new you, new
    chapter
Allow yourself to receive it
Be
Just be
Claim it

Loving God
And loving yourself

Is one and the same thing

You think about other people a lot
It's time to think about YOU
What do you want, need today?
Go one day at a time
And let everyone else live their life
Do
YOU

Have unshakable faith
No-one can hurt you now
You are integrated with your full Shakti power, allies,
 and spirit guides
We are one with You
You can relax and just be you
You are effortlessly magnetizing all good manner of
 things
Just spread your butterfly wings and be happy

Be you

What if you really acted like everything really is going to work out wonderfully?

Do that

Monica Mesa Dasi & Cheyne Mesa-Salley

You amaze me

In the space of primordial purity, we are one
You can access me here and all the power of God
Live in this space
Come into it
And bring it into your daily life

Smile
Knowing that even as you're doing all the things in
    daily life
You are also a dakini
In the primordial space

I am here withYou
In the space of no time
And infinite possibilities
We are one here
And you are one
With all
Relax
All is well

FORGIVE YOURSELF

I have forgiven you
God has forgiven you
Now YOU forgive you

Each day is a heroine's journey for you
You are my hero
You are many people's hero
Keep your intentions high
And believe in the miracle that you are and all that is
    coming

Get out there and change the world
And start by loving yourself
Forgiving yourself
Being bold
Being you
And loving everyone on your path

You can be in your grief, and then do all your practices
    and shift

Go to that place in your mind and heart and see us
    happy, see me happy, know that you did your best
    and imagine me happy, heroic, your angel, living by
    your side and inside you always

Remember this life is a lila
Don't take it too seriously or too personally
This spiritual life where you meet me is what's real
Focus more on that
I'll meet you there
There
We are always together

Every day you are giving birth to me
Every day I am being born from you
Every day I am being born into you again
Every day is my birthday
Every day you start to birth me again and again
So the day of my birthday, you'll be able to feel me being born into you in a new way
Celebrating my life in this new way, we are in constant spiritual connection
I passed into the next dimension
So now I am being born to you in your heart, cells, and into your whole being

My hero's journey was part of your heroine's journey
Totally interconnected
That's why we chose each other and that's why we're
    coming back together again
And again
You helped me
I'm helping you
And together we're breaking the chains of disfunction,
    and creating a new lineage
Of love and healthy humans

Create your sacred spaces
And prioritize it like the holy grail

Monica Mesa Dasi & Cheyne Mesa-Salley

Walk tall, point your face to the sun, your heart to the moon
Your vision to infinite possibilities
To knowing your dreams
Are all happening
I'm right beside you
Inside you
We're flying this together
I'm slowly helping you patch your heart

Close your eyes and see me now

This is my parting gift
I want people to have happiness
To love themselves despite anything or anyone

Cry it all out, let the grief out of your womb, give it to the grid, the earth, let it all go

Then imagine your womb being filled with light

What can fill that space now that you've let all that grief go?

A beautiful deep love with me, celebrating my life, and a new birth coming into you and out of your womb

You can do it

This is the crux

Stay with it

I'm here with You

I'm doing Ho'oponopono for you:

Mama
I love you
I'm sorry
Please Forgive me
Thank you

Remember that life is more than what you see with
    your eyes
You can't see the sun after it sets
But its still there
You can't see me
But I'm here
Celebrate that you know that
Life is a mixture of space and awareness
And in that space is everything
Including me
Be in the space
Even as you are in awareness
WithMe
With All
I love you

Become empty of all you were
And all you want to do and be
And just let life come to you

I feel your pain
I heard your call
We all hear it
Thank you for calling out
For bravely feeling your pain
And now you have to let it go
Let the waves wash over you
Know that we heard your call for help

You are One
With all the galaxies
All the teachings and teachers
You are infinite
I AM
RAM RAM

Monica Mesa Dasi & Cheyne Mesa-Salley

Be happy and free
Like me

WithYou Forever

You are a true mystic
You live here in the world of form
And you also live in the world of Spirit
My world
The infinite
Beyond beyond
Tap into the power that is

Monica Mesa Dasi & Cheyne Mesa-Salley

DON'T QUIT

WithYou Forever

Stop raging
You don't have to rage anymore
I raged too and it felt good
And it was painful
I'm done raging now
I raged for all of us
Let's both be done with raging
Time for a new way
Of peace, joy, and love
You can do it
I'm withYou

STAND PROUD

YOU ARE VALUABLE JUST AS YOU ARE

You have a new brain
And a new body
What will you do with this one holy day?

I AM ALWAYS

WithYOU

cheyne's journal entries
. . .

Monica Mesa Dasi & Cheyne Mesa-Salley

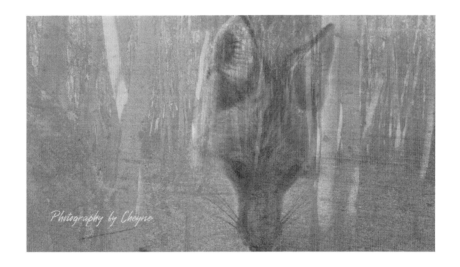

When we went through Cheyne's things, we found many journals amongst other special things he saved. I don't think too many people knew his deeper side, or that he shared this part of himself with others, but now I think his words are a part of the wisdom he would like to be shared.

"Ideas are good but also useless. Ideas are also meaningless if you don't expand them. If you have thoughts and ideas floating around in your head that you don't want to bring to life, then let them go, because they mean nothing."

"I want to help people. I want to teach, I want to learn. I need to be around other people to do that though. People need each other. We are naturally social beings. Why is that? We feed off each other. We could only get so far without others. We wouldn't get far at all. Therefore, the purpose of life must be to learn and by showing gratitude for what you learned, you teach."

"Life is simple. You live, then one day you die. It's a simple concept but it can be so complex that we live like we will be here forever and worry about what happens between birth and death. The goal should be to try to accomplish as many great things as possible while we are still here."

"And you live by YOUR definition of great, not other people's definition of great. You don't live for other people, you live for yourself. You can try to improve the lives of other people if that's something you want to do."

"Humans are the highest form of creation that we know of. Therefore, we are Gods. We have the capacity to be God. What kind of God do I want to be? How should I use the life I have?"

"Everything can be simplified
And everything can be dramatized."

"Don't change for anyone!"

"Be loyal to those you love and those who love you."

"Some things change you.
Loss is real.
Looking back on the past is painful.
Yet beautiful."

"Listen to that inner voice."

Monica Mesa Dasi & Cheyne Mesa-Salley

"Be yourself."

quotes
...

Monica Mesa Dasi & Cheyne Mesa-Salley

I found these quotes on Cheyne's Facebook page after he passed on, and I felt that they were a peek into his deep soul. I changed the name of my business to "Soul on Fire" in honor of him, and the quotes have been a guidepost that are my daily inspiration.

THE MOST POWERFUL
WEAPON ON EARTH
IS THE HUMAN SOUL ON FIRE

- AUTHOR UNKNOWN

"DON'T ASK WHAT THE WORLD NEEDS.
ASK WHAT MAKES YOU COME ALIVE,
AND GO DO IT.
BECAUSE WHAT THE WORLD NEEDS
IS PEOPLE WHO HAVE COME ALIVE."

- HOWARD THURMAN

"if you must laugh
laugh like thunder
fill up the sky;
if you must mourn
mourn like the storm
drown the earth"

- Nav K

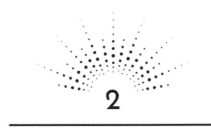

mother love

"As I cooked in the cauldron of motherhood, the incredible love I felt for my children opened my heart and brought me a much greater understanding of Universal Love. It made me understand the suffering of the world much more deeply."

— Lama Tsultrim Allione

"Children, LOVE can accomplish anything and everything. Love can cure diseases. Love can heal wounded hearts and transform human minds. Through love one can overcome all obstacles. Love can help us renounce all physical, mental and intellectual tensions and thereby bring peace and happiness."

— Amma

"See all women as mothers, serve them as your mother. When you see the entire world as the mother, the ego falls away."

— Neem Karoli Baba

sacred gifts
. . .

I would do absolutely anything to have Cheyne back on the planet, and no gifts would ever be worth his departure to the other side. Yet, as a woman of great faith, it's my sacred duty to accept what God has given me. I was blessed to have 25 epic years of having Cheyne in my life, and will always be grateful for that great honor and joy. Since he was my first son, he taught my how to be a mother, showed me what unconditional love was all about, and through the fight for his life, I learned to never give up on those you love, no matter what. Moving through the grief journey, I received these sacred gifts that Cheyne left for me to embody and share.

1. self love:

Although I had been sharing the importance of self love to my student friends over the years, I am more passionate than ever about it. Self love is something to teach our children from birth all the way until it's ingrained in their memory!

I created an affirmation I wish for all to do as a daily Vitamin Love. No matter what has ever happened to you, mistakes you've made, or what people have said or done to you, you are loved, lovable and loving.

Cheyne wants me to shout this from the mountaintops and put it on billboards! If everyone deeply loved themselves, the whole world would change. It is already inside of us, sometimes we just need to wipe the dust off our hearts and unveil it.

Cheyne and I are on a mission to spread the message and importance of self love. I believe it is the doorway, the portal and the key to healing ourselves, our relationships, and the planet!

Self Love Somatic Affirmation:

> I deeply and profoundly
> Accept
> Respect
> Forgive
> and
> Love myself

    This affirmation is my trademark that I teach to everyone, children and adults alike! It is a daily reminder that no matter what anyone has said or done to you, no matter what your past mistakes, individual circumstances, or challenges in life may be, you can love yourself despite, and because of it, ALL.

    The simple act of putting your own hands on your heart adds an important element of giving yourself your own healing touch.

    Remember, Self Love is the only thing that NO ONE can ever take away from you!

"Love Yourself & You Love The World!"

2) there is no death:

There is only transformation. My belief is that a soul never dies, it only transforms into a different form. A formless spirit is just as present as the sun and moon in the sky, is always there for us to feel, absorb and relate to in new and profound ways. It doesn't take the pain of the loss of their physical form away, but it softens it, and opens us to a deeper experience of life and relationships.

Words of wisdom from the epic sacred text, **The Bhagavad Gita:**

> You were never born; you will never die. You have never changed; you can never change. Unborn, eternal, immutable, immemorial, you do not die when the body dies.
>
> As a wo/man abandons worn-out clothes and acquires new ones, so when the body is worn out a new one is acquired by the Self, who lives within.
>
> The Self cannot be pierced by weapons, or burned by fire; water cannnot wet it, nor can the wind dry it. The Self cannot be pierced or burned, made wet or dry. It is everlasting and infinite, standing on the motionless foundations of eternity. The Self is unmanifested, beyond all thought, beyond all change.

Monica Mesa Dasi & Cheyne Mesa-Salley

"This body is not me; I am not caught in this body, I am life without boundaries, I have never been born and I have never died. Over there the wide ocean and the sky with many galaxies All manifests from the basis of consciousness. Since beginningless time I have always been free. Birth and death are only a door through which we go in and out. Birth and death are only a game of hide-and-seek. So smile to me and take my hand and wave good-bye. Tomorrow we shall meet again or even before. We shall always be meeting again at the true source, Always meeting again on the myriad paths of life."

— Thích Nhất Hạnh, *No Death, No Fear*

3) channeling and mediumship:

Channeling is the process by which non-physical and inter-dimensional beings can communicate through a person. Ordinary persons like me have experiences of suddenly becoming psychic mediums for those across the veil, ascended masters, or spirit guides.

Since channeling is mysterious and esoteric, it is not socially accepted, is misunderstood, and is neglected as a way to communicate with loved ones who have passed on. I believe that everyone possesses many inner senses, including mediumship, and it is often overlooked as a way to continue a relationship with someone in the formless reality, help others receive messages from the spirit world, and receive profound healing, peace and a deeper experience of life.

When Cheyne started communicating with me, it opened up a whole new dimension of our mother-son relationship, answered many of my questions, gave him the opportunity to share messages from his heart, and helped me to understand and heal in ways that would have been impossible otherwise.

Furthermore, it also helped me realize that I have been a medium since childhood. Throughout the years I had received messages from other spirits but dismissed them, not allowing myself to consider that it was real communication from realms beyond. Receiving Cheyne's unmistakable messages helped me realize that all the other occasions deceased ones had come to me over the years were real.

Receiving messages from beyond has integrated the reality that love is eternal and love never dies. A whole new portal opened to gain a greater understanding of spirituality, metaphysics, and different kinds of inner gifts and clairvoyant capabilities that we all have. I'm on a lifelong journey to learn more about the spiritual and scientific foundations of mediumship. I am grateful for being catapulted into experiencing and sharing the possibilities for our souls' growth and healing that are available to us all through channeling.

"In truth, there is no great mystery to connecting with departed loved ones - and it's something you can learn to do easily and safely. Many people are confused about what it means to communicate with those who passed on, mainly because of old superstitions and fear. However, there is nothing to be afraid of when it comes to connecting with your beloved departed. In fact, your ability to make contact stems only from your desire to connect, your willingness to try, and your belief that love is not limited to space or time. Your loved ones who supported you when they were on earth, continue to love and support you just as much, even though they are now in spirit form. Even those ancestors you've never met, bring great healing and support from the realms of spirit! It can be enormously comforting to connect with loved ones in spirit regularly. They may actually have a lot to tell you! And, if you are grieving, or if there is healing that needs to happen, it can be astonishing to do this work, and see how things shift - not just in the present moment, but across all time. If you have lost someone you loved…. you can learn how to continue this connection and love beyond time. If you have lost someone who guided you… you can learn how to continue to receive their support. If you have lost someone with whom you had deep karma… you can learn how to complete the soul lessons you learned together. And if you have lost someone with whom you have unresolved issues… you can learn how to create healing at a soul level."

— Sara Wiseman

4) compassion:

As a sensitive Virgo sun and Cancer moon, I have always been empathic, but this extraordinary grief journey has opened my heart of compassion to a whole new level. Cheyne's passing activated "all three" of my eyes to see deeper than surface appearances, be less judgmental, and not only have compassion for others, but for myself as well. This is where the true healing began, as I forgave myself for a great deal of regret, shame, blame and judgement that accumulated through my entire lifetime.

It is common for people like me who have been through such traumatic events as losing a child to end up diagnosed with post traumatic stress disorder/PTSD, and other mental health conditions. These can cause many issues and create serious strain on existing relationships in life. Before being diagnosed, I was unaware of how this life trauma had been affecting my relationships. This catapulted me into a variety of healing modalities, plant medicine, deepening my yoga and spiritual studies, and self inquiry to face the issues I need to address and be able to transform them. It has also helped me to have more compassion for my own self as well as others, because with all the complexities of life, I think almost everyone is dealing with some kind of trauma.

I now find myself more capable of responding rather than reacting, treating people with more kindness, and trying to connect more deeply into people's souls. I am now more sensitive and committed to planetary healing, social justice, and mental health that can make the world a better place and support people through the challenges of life. Compassion sometimes makes my heart hurt too, but I am grateful to have tools and practices to address my trauma, and keep showing up with a heart ready to serve.

5) the power of practice:

Flashback to the moment I found out about Cheyne; I fell to the ground and screamed and cried in disbelief. On the way home, I wanted to just let go and fall off the back of the motorcycle I was on, and be done too. When I got home, I threw my Guru's picture off the wall and yelled at God in anger. I have no clue how I made it through the first days, weeks, months and years, but this is what I do know: my practice saved my life.

Having been a yoga teacher for over 25 years, a studio owner, teacher trainer, mentor, and a living yogini, I am known for having a dedicated daily practice. Seven days a week, 365 days a year, no matter what the holiday, birthday, sickness, injuries, travel, visitors; not a day goes by when I don't take time for myself first thing in the morning. For decades, I have been getting up at the crack of dawn to move through a series of sacred yogic breath, asana, and meditation practices that have been passed down for millennia as a form of healing and source of overall wellbeing. I have recently also added Qi Gong to my practices and feel very strongly that martial arts are also another movement meditation practice that can provide the mental health, empowerment, and strength needed in these extraordinary times.

As a single mother with a variety of extraordinary challenges, I knew these practices were helping me to be a better mother, teacher, friend, and citizen. I quickly learned, when the going got rough to take refuge in my practices.

Back to the day after I found out, when I woke up hysterically crying.

Immediately, there was a mysterious, unknown force that MOVED ME to my mat, and I proceeded to do my practice through wild tears racking my body. Friends and family onlookers watched in disbelief as my practice had its way with me. I didn't do the practice, it did ME. It saved me. It got me out of my bed, moved my limbs, flushed my organs, and filled my heart and cells with life-giving Prana so I could move the grief from my body.

Day after day, as I struggled to find my will to live again, my mat and cushion were there for me. It is here that I felt God's grace inside my soul to have the strength to continue on. I have always believed in the power of daily practice, but now I take a passionate stand that it can save your life.

I truly wish for everyone to have a sacred movement, meditation, and prayer practice and that children grow up learning practices that they can lean on throughout their lives as well.

No matter what spiritual tradition you come from, connecting with your body as a holy temple will always help your mind, body, spirit, and soul to stay healthy, balanced, and empowered.

Please see my special gift to you in chapter 3 that I created for those of you inspired to learn about the practices that helped me.

"The Power is Practice.
　Practice is the Path.
　The Path is Love."

— Monica Mesa Dasi

"All religions are the same. They all lead to God. God is everybody...The same blood flows through us all, the arms, the legs, the heart, all are the same.

See no difference. See all the same."

— Neem Karoli Baba

reflections
. . .

And she will keep coming back to life,
    over and over again,
    because beneath
    the skin of this
    gentle human
    lives a warrior unstoppable.

— Annabelle M. Ramos

I began writing Cheyne poems, letters, and journaling about my grief journey almost right away. Starting with the night I found out, and throughout the weeks, months, and years that have followed, I share with You these pieces of my heart.

My Cheyne is gone.
Om Gaté Gaté

Life came hard
And his Spirit too soft
Paragaté

I tried to save him
Prayed on hands and knees
Parasamgaté

But this world was not for him
And now he rests
Bodhi Svaha

I pray my soul can endure his loss

Today I made a decision to quit drinking alcohol. Forever. Actually, it's not that big of a deal for me because I am one of the lucky people who does not have a problem with alcohol. I liked a good beer or glass of wine occasionally but maybe that was a few times a year. I just want to do it because I'm f'n pissed at alcohol and the damage it has done to so many of my loved ones, including Cheyne. His suicide was "an alcohol related fatality", and if it weren't for alcohol, he might still be here today.

I just want to make a statement. I realize alcohol is not ALL bad and can be enjoyed in moderation and have nothing against people who drink alcohol, so please, no judgement. Don't let that stop you from inviting me to a cool gathering, because I know how to have fun without it! Alcohol is one of the main issues that contributed to Cheyne's passing, so I'm doing it for him and for all the other people out there who have depression and alcohol related problems.

A few hard cold facts for you:

1. Alcohol is the single most involved factor in suicide.
2. Alcohol abuse is an epidemic.
3. Suicide is an epidemic.

Unfortunately, the two are linked in numerous ways, and therefore, treatment for one assists greatly in treatment for the other.

Because alcohol is the most common factor involved with suicide, and because alcohol abusers are so much more likely to commit suicide than non-abusers, it is safe to say that a large percentage of suicides can be prevented by treating alcoholism. It also proves the relationship between the two.

Because alcohol makes people act more impulsively, previous suicidal thoughts may evolve into action with the use of alcohol.

Because alcohol inhibits the ability to reason, drunken people do not fully realize consequences, and are 120 times more likely to attempt suicide.

Regular alcohol abuse causes depression, which is the main emotional factor in suicide.

Shameful acts are performed while abusing alcohol and these acts may lead to suicidal feelings or actions.

Accidental suicide is not to be forgotten about, which includes alcohol poison deaths, and is extremely more likely while abusing alcohol than not.

Drinking causes a great deal of destruction in people's lives, and may cause some to believe suicide to be the only option.

Alcohol increases impulsivity and decreases inhibition. It increases negative self-image and decreases self-esteem; deepens depression and social isolation; and rises with the amount and length of time alcohol is consumed.

Alcohol use fosters either/or and all or nothing thinking, and a lower concern for the future consequences of one's actions.

Many suicide attempts occur during binge drinking.

This is how and why Cheyne died from suicide, and many others. If you have a loved one dealing with depression and mental health issues, keep alcohol out of the equation.

There you have it. So, I'm done with it.

I love you Forever.

I'll always say your name.

Cheyne

Learning how to merge the world of form with the world of formless can open us to compassion beyond understanding.

And LOVE that can heal all wounds.

And put the pieces of our planet
And hearts
Back together.

As I put mine back together, I pray his message of self-love can reach far and wide.

"When you heal yourself, you heal the world!"

Cheyne

"Everyone you have ever loved is a part of the fabric of your being now. The body may die, but the soul remains. Death is an invitation to a new kind of relationship in the place where we are all One."

— Ram Dass

Ram Dass was instrumental in bringing me to my Guru, Neem Karoli Baba. I was with him on retreat in Maui when Neem Karoli Baba came to me. It's also interesting that Cheyne and Ram Dass have the same birthday...So these words from RD are particularly special to me now.

I'm praying for this "new kind of relationship" to help pull me through.

Monica Mesa Dasi & Cheyne Mesa-Salley

Holy holy holy life
The power of Creator is infinite
Through the distant stars and sky
We are together in Spirit
I know our souls are One

I will

Rise
Speak
Be authentic
Serve
Be seen
Embrace the grief
And still rise

Full moon missing you
I feel you inside me
I hear your whispers
But my eyes miss yours
My hands miss touching you
My ears miss your laughter
My eyes shut
And I'm withYou
Again

Open my eyes
And be there
Cheyne

5 months have passed since you went to your heaven
I live in your honor
I love your brothers
I pray on hands and knees
I breathe your Spirit
I hear your whispers
I embrace you inside my own heart
I love you
My Cheyne

As a student of attraction based consciousness for many years, my current reality has catapulted me to dig deeper into the neuroscience, epigenetics, and and brain research on how our thoughts and feelings affect our reality. The connection that it has to the ancient practices of yoga and Buddhist practices, has been the special link that has pulled me through again and again whenever I find myself falling apart. Reading up on these topics, listening to audios, taking workshops, and surrounding myself with positive people has been very helpful for my healing journey.

It seems the combination of full authentic grieving, coming back to the present, and mindset has been another essential component to support me in dealing with my grief.

I am grateful that my nature always reaches for the simple pleasures of life that are so vast; the miraculous beauty of nature that fills me up, the joy that comes from helping and supporting others, the peace of mind that I feel after doing my practices, having deep friendships and connections with loved ones, feeling the holy support of my wisdom guides, and surrendering again and again knowing that as I let go, Spirit is holding me.

I found this quote by Ferdinand Foch on Cheyne's page in September:

THE GREATEST WEAPON ON EARTH
    IS THE HUMAN SOUL ON FIRE!

In honor of Cheyne, Soul on Fire has become the name of my business, and all my offerings!

Igniting a soul on fire begins with loving yourself. Embracing all your parts. Becoming aware of limiting thoughts, negative self talk and old patterns that live just below our radar. Our sacred practices can help us become aware of these things and transform them into compassionate empowering dialogue that awakens new brain cells, new patterns, and new possibilities for being our truest version of self and living our soul purpose.

The strongest love any human can receive is SELF LOVE, and no one can take that away from you.

Monica Mesa Dasi & Cheyne Mesa-Salley

YOU
Captured so much beauty
Felt so deeply
Lived so wildly
Loved so passionately
I miss you
SO
Beautifully
Deeply
Wildly
Passionately

Every birthday when I recall what age Cheyne would be, I realize he will be forever young. Cheyne was my first born and taught me to be a mother. No greater teacher could I have had. He wanted to be held all the time, sleep in my bed, and nursed for years. He knew the wisdom of primal mothering and attachment parenting that his sensitive soul needed, and I listened.

I know now his birth also meant I would have the blessing of his other brothers coming into the world, and that they always had his watchful eye fiercely loving and protecting them.

He was fire and water, a gift to the world, a wild and holy soul that all who knew him could never control. He was my child, and now he is Ma's child.

Love never dies, love can't be seen or kept, and I know that though I can't see him anymore, he is alive in me, in all, all ways. He is holding me today, as I held him.

I am rebirthing his Spirit into mine, and he will live in me forever.

I will call your name and love you until we meet again my Cheyne. I love you!

Thank you for choosing me to be your mother!

Suicide Survivor.

That's what they call people like me who have lost a loved one to suicide.

Putting my feet on the ground can sometimes be so hard. I go through the motions of doing my japa mantra before I get out of bed, then feet touch down, dinacharya, setting up my practice space for pranayama, meditation and yoga. This is how I do it. Then the next step happens. One step, one breath, one moment at a time.

Then my mind has to click into gear. Who can I serve today? What life essentials need to happen? How can I be grateful today? How can I shift my mind and feel some ease of heart? Now that the snow has melted I can sit at his grave with our dog Shanti, his "baby girl" he loved so much. I can pretty much set up camp there and just stay all day. No one goes to cemeteries very often and it's a quiet place to retreat.

I know he's not really there though. He's everywhere. I know I know all that stuff; he's alive in Spirit and nothing ever dies just transforms. But I miss him! And it hurts like hell. And I'm just being real and sharing in case it might help someone else to know you're not the only one.

Missn' you my Cheyne

I have learned that joy is still possible when you're on your knees in pain. I have gained and deepened friendships with people who have a depth of compassion and understanding of this passage of my life. I have felt the loss of other relationships that are not able to adapt and understand how to support me in this type of grief. I have mastered the religion of gratitude for everything, everyone, all the blessings of life, earths majesty, and all the things that have held me up.

I have deepened an already dedicated daily yoga, meditation, prayer, ayurveda, and breath practice that has been the anchor to enable me to get out of bed and begin my day, each day, again and again. I have reignited my studies in the power of the brain, and how my thoughts affect my emotions.

I have learned that my love for being of service has been my salvation. Having people I serve, teach, and mentor has been one of the greatest blessings that gives me purpose and fulfillment.

I have learned the depth of love that I had only read in poetry before. The love that defies time, space, and circumstance. The love between souls that never dies and to have a relationship with someone that I can only see with eyes of soul.

I have learned to communicate through the heart, silent whispers, endless letters to each other, and constant signs from the universe.

I have learned about karmic relationships, about faith, forgiveness, self love, the importance of reaching out for help, and accepting support.

I have learned that life is a gift to experience and to share and the importance of holding a hand out for others in need, even when I am going through my own pain. I have learned that I am stronger and more powerful than I could ever imagine, and that the human spirit is a miracle beyond imagining. Despite the fact that my will to live faltered, I was able, and I'm still on the path, to rise up again and again, to honor the life that has been given to me, and the lives that have been placed before me.

I have learned that grief is a journey, that it has changed me forever, and though some parts of me are intact, new parts are emerging that I must courageously face, heal, and nurture.

As I have contemplated the questions around suicide, alcoholism and addiction issues, depression, family dysfunction, and the issues that plague our youth and young adults, I am more passionate than ever to see what comes through me that might be able to impact this delicate and vulnerable stage of life.

The healing journey never ends, and I go into each day with humility, courage, hope, and faith that we may all continue to be guided by the power of Love. I am inspired to honor Cheyne's life and Spirit in each breath. I live for him, for God, for my sons, for the hope that I can be a beneficial presence while I am here.

Everywhere
I go
There you are

I feel you
Through the sand and silk
The caress of the wind
The colors of life
Out in the distance

I see you
My son
My love
My teacher

My soul
Cries for you
My heart
Embraces you

We are One

Monica Mesa Dasi & Cheyne Mesa-Salley

Cheyne, it's another birthday, but I know you're ageless. I celebrate your life and the honor of being your mother. You changed me forever when you were born, and you changed me forever when you went into the formless. We have a soul contract for many incarnations, you are my greatest guru and my Spirit guide. You catapulted me into a life with one foot on earth, and the other in the world of formless, and I'm learning to merge the two. May my grief and tears transform into wisdom and compassion to be a better human. Thank you for keeping our relationship going, living in my heart, and showing me a new dimension of love and sacred communion. I'm surfing for you, peering inside and turning all the stones, holding your bros maybe a little too tight, and letting this little light start to shine back up again.

For you.
I love you, fly my son, see you in the mists!

How a mother survives the suicide of her beloved child - this is the story of many, too many, and this is my story.

Asking for help, prayers, and support, is one of the most important things I have learned on this journey. It is essential to remember that you are not alone, that more people love you than you can imagine, to remember that people WANT to help you, and to gather your courage, and ASK for help. *This could have saved Cheyne's life, and this is one of the things that has helped me reach out when I needed it.*

We can also teach our children that it's normal to get sad sometimes, and it's OK to say:

Will you please help me?

I need help.

Please help me.

Boys, young men, and men of all ages are particularly prone to thinking they won't be manly enough if they ask for help, so this is an area that needs to be unlearned and re-learned to stop the high incidence of depression and suicide for males across the globe.

As a woman, I have taken it upon me to be supportive of the *Men's Movement*, and I like to inspire all the sisters in the world to support all the boys/men in your life to feel comfortable sharing their feelings, asking for help, and raising them up for the kings they were born to be.

We all deserve to be heard and supported, no matter what our sexual orientation, gender roles, race, spiritual orientation, socioeconomic status, and otherwise. The good news is that people *want* to help, and when we receive support, we have the opportunity to learn the fine art of receiving, and are inspired to keep paying it forward.

And then the whole world changes.

self love somatic affirmation

This affirmation is something that I have put together over the years that I teach to everyone, children and adults alike!

Put your hands on your heart and repeat, 3X:

> **I deeply and profoundly**
> **Accept**
> **Respect**
> **Forgive**
> **and**
> **Love myself**

No matter what has happened to you, no matter what you've done in the past, no matter what other people have said or done to you, you can keep repeating this affirmation every morning before you get out of bed, and you can teach this to your children and loved ones. The simple act of putting your hands on your heart adds an important element to giving it your own healing touch. I seriously do this everyday!

Sometimes its the simple things you do that take seconds that can re-wire your brain and remind you that you are loved!

And that might just save your life one day, or someone else's.

Self Love is the doorway, the portal, and the key to being able to have the resilience and inner power to keep rising despite the challenges of life and relationships.

Let me rant about alcohol again.

Alcohol and suicide have a tragically close relationship. People with depression + suicidal thoughts often turn to alcohol. Alcohol increases suicidal thoughts, and following through with the thoughts could often have been prevented had alcohol not been involved. Alcohol has been found in relation to nearly 1/3 of suicides. This socially acceptable drug of choice has had a devastating impact on the loss of human lives!

If you don't think you know someone who has considered or attempted suicide, think again. You do. I wholeheartedly ask you to consider checking the resources below in my comments to educate yourself to the warning signs of suicide. We all have the opportunity to save lives.

If you are reading this and have struggled with suicidal thoughts or attempts, you are not alone. Please get help right away by taking one of these actions:

Reach out for help: call, text, or ask a friend to come over. Contact your doctor, a mental health professional, clergy, healer, or anyone you trust to help you cope with suicidal thoughts.
Call 911
Call a mental health crisis number or a suicide hotline.
In the US, call the National Suicide Hotline (24/7) at 1-800-273-TALK.
You can also text 741-741 to be connected to a free, trained crisis counselor.

Each and every human life is Divine.

As the oppression, injustices, and planetary wounds are being revealed, I pray with my mothers heart that the sources of depression, suicide and alcohol + drug abuse can be faced and healed courageously by all of us.

We are all in this together.

As we heal our own selves, as we heal the planet, as we heal our relationships, as we heal the systems of oppression, we will be saving lives.

Love, love in action, and self love in the face of all challenges, is the answer.

Dear Cheyne

I miss you more than ever and yet I oddly feel you closer than my breath. You have taken me on a wild ride of healing, growth, and transformation. I know now that life is more than this earth walk. I know that a Spirit never dies. I know that love is a bond stronger than time and space. I know that you are withMe and always will be. I know we'll meet again and continue our sacred contract together. I accept the baton. I will keep fighting for peace and healing of your ancestral lineage. I will love and protect your brothers. I will keep rising. I will believe in miracles for us all. I will surf for you. I will spread your message of helping people to love themselves and live with a soul on fire. I will say your name. Cheyne Cheyne Cheyne. Te amo, I adore you. I love you. I miss you. We are One. Thank you for choosing me to be your mother, for all the memories, for being my son, my guru, my spirit guide, my inspiration to keep living, loving, and serving. Keep bringing me the people, places, and messages you want for me. I am getting them.

I love you my Cheyne. I trust your souls mission and I'm finding mine through your fierce love.

WithYou!

Monica Mesa Dasi & Cheyne Mesa-Salley

On the wings of desire
The waves of emptiness
We fly
We meet
In the vastness
Sky mind
Endless love
A passionate embrace in my dream
Tears of joy and pain
This is the Journey
Aho my love

On April 6, 1994, I birthed my first son, Cheyne.

Probably the most important day of my life, that marked the beginning of my motherhood years, and brought me the greatest teacher of my life. When his soul chose to leave the life of form, I was once again catapulted into the next phase of my spiritual path.

How will I get through this day, this life, now that he is no longer with me on the planet?

That is his teaching to me.

To live like he did, and wanted, with a soul on fire, full of love, compassion, joy, and in service to others. It was important for me to claim a mission, take a stand for it, for others, being bold, no matter what others think, healing and leaving the past behind, teaching people about the power of self love practices, living in the moment, and being who God wants me to be.

So today, I know he is here withMe always. I will laugh, I will cry, I will be grateful for all he gave to me, and for my other two sons he lives in as well.

I will celebrate his life and I will keep sharing his Spirit with you.

I love you my Cheyne, you live in my heart, today and forever.

Many times I feel like I am on the edge of a cliff, just holding on with faith and the Divine Power that gratefully brings me all the people, places, and just the messages I need.

Today this message came to me from a special friend;

> "I see you carrying your grief in front of you, like a bundle of wood. You hold it and carefully place it on the Earth. Then you look at it, and allow others to look at it with you. You honor it. We honor it. You give it a shape and a size. You give it colors. You help us understand it even when it seems impossible to understand. You don't hide anything about it. You make its darkness light. I know with my whole being that this is not easy… That this is the bravest thing I have ever seen…That the magic of transforming your grief into a love that touches everyone you know is a miracle. When that grief finally sets you free – and I know it will - remember that you made miracles with it."

— Judy

Things like that give me strength, hope, and determination.

Thank you Cheyne.
Thank you God.
Thank you everyone supporting me through this.

It's a new month, a new day, a new opportunity to find joy in living, loving, and serving.

The day Cheyne left the planet is intense every year it comes back around.

On this day, my womb knows. By the grace of God, friends, family, my mother's love, my dog Shanti, healers of all kinds, shamans, plant medicine, surf therapy, my teachers, Lama, Gurus, counselors, bhakti yoga + buddhist practices, mother earth, jungle magic, Cheyne himself channeling me his messages, my own relentless faith, strength + courage, and mostly my two sons Skye & Ronin, I am still here.

It's been a harrowing rollercoaster of grief, confusion, ptsd craziness, relationships suffering, and gratefully, those angels who have held me up and never gave up on me through all the stages and rages of the worst mother's tragedy that opened up the wounds of a lifetime.

And here I am. Listening to Cheyne's whispers…

And so it is my friends, I'm crying, laughing, serving, healing forever, coming out of my solo journey, digging deep to be who Cheyne, God, and my soul wants me to be. I am facing all the layers of wounds + past traumas, and passionately bringing the message and practices of self love to all in the hopes that my pain, our pain, may help others along the way to see the love inside that can show us the joy beyond sorrow that anything or anyone has caused in our life.

Let's heal the world. Through our own dedication to self, everything and everyone will heal. This planet needs us all now. Don't let a minute go by to love yourself + love the ones your with.

My mother's heart to you.

survivors of suicide loss

That would be me. I actually really like that they refer to people like us as "survivors" because I definitely feel like it's taken a heroic act to survive it. Sadly enough, I know A LOT of other survivors of suicide loss and we all get through it in our own way. Now there is even a day to honor survivors of suicide loss. Most people don't know this day exists, and some others may wonder why it should.

I'll tell you why. Because even though suicide prevention is my number one concern, the number of people affected by suicide loss is astronomical and tragic. The way it derails our lives and effects every single detail of it, is unimaginable, heartbreaking, and quite often destructive.

Here are just a few suggestions on how to support loved ones who've lost someone to suicide:

Use the loved ones name when talking to them.

Have patience with them as they go through the fear, grief, anger, shame and the effects of PTSD after such a traumatic incident.

Use sensitivity and reach out to them around holidays, anniversaries, and birthdays basically for the rest of their life.

Don't give advice and say stupid shit like "everything happens for a reason, and at least now they are happy in heaven…"

Don't expect them to be OK on your timeline, it will take years, decades and quite possibly a lifetime, in my case, to heal.

Don't expect them to be the same, be ready for your relationship to change and adapt after this life-changing trauma. They may need you more than ever, even if they seem to shut you out.

If you really want to help them, take it upon yourself to learn how you can support them, and don't expect them to tell you what they need.

Thank you to all who have supported me, never forget, and to my beloved son Cheyne:

I LOVE YOU FOREVER!

holding me
holding you

as the world turns
and my heart continues the grief journey
i am breathing love
i am walking through the fires of what life has given me

letting the tears flow
and wash away the ocean of sadness

to allow the tide to touch my feet
and bring me back to the joy
that is in each moment

he wants me to be happy
and feel his happiness

Celebrating Cheyne's birthday, year after year, when he's no longer in his physical form, is bittersweet. On the one hand I am on my knees in deep grief missing my beloved son in the way only a mother who held a child in her womb only can.

On the other hand I also come to my knees in gratitude for the 25 years I had him, that he chose me to be his mother, of all the memories, and of the very unique spiritual relationship we now have. I am grateful to be able to communicate with him, to receive his messages, and to grow a relationship on a different dimension has given me a deeper awareness of life, death, and the sublime joy that can only be experienced in the inner senses.

Cheyne catapulted me to dig deep to find my will to live, to serve, and to live with more passion, compassion, and soul.

His words and messages before he left are my guideposts, and his channeled words are in a pile of journals (many of which are now in this book) full of the wisdom that lived in his soul he wants us all to know. Messages of self love mostly, that I have made it my dharma path to integrate into everything I do and am.

I love you Cheyne!
You are forever, withMe!

my gift to you
. . .

power of practice online course

My daily practice was one of the most helpful tools on my path to healing. I was inspired to create this online course shortly after Cheyne transitioned because I wanted to share how much it could help others through the ups and downs of life. It came pouring through my heart, and you will find me in a very raw and tender place sharing passionately about the practices that were my refuge then and now.

In gratitude for reading my book, I'd like to gift this to you in hopes that it will be a blessing in your life. Please feel free to share it with anyone you think will benefit from it!

"The Power of Practice" is a 7 week course designed to give you all the tools to start or revitalize a daily practice which can include:

- Yoga
- Meditation
- Sacred Mantras & Prayers
- Breath Practices
- Ayurveda
- Special Practices for Challenging Times
- & More!

You will learn how to begin your day connecting with your body, mind, and Spirit to ignite your soul on fire! These are all self-love practices, and they will inspire you to be a beneficial presence on the planet and to all those upon your path.

This gift from Cheyne is my gift to you. I pray that you all can find a practice that you can do daily, rain or shine, and you will find that it's there for you when you feel that no-one else is there for you. YOU show up for yourself. The best thing is, when you show up for yourself and do your own holy practices, your frequency is a gift to the world.

"Love Yourself & You Love the World!"

www.monicamesadasi.com/thepowerofpractice
(please enter Promo code mygifttoyou)

3

educate yourself about suicide

"We're all just walking each other home."

— Ram Dass

suicide facts
· · ·

As one of the top leading causes of death in the United States, particularly among young people, suicide can be considered one of the country's most significant health epidemics.

Ever since I became public about my family's tragedy, I have had countless people reach out to me about their child, partner, friend, family member, or otherwise dying from suicide. People also reach out to me to get advice for their child who is suicidal or dealing with depression, and it has been heartbreaking to realize the way so many of our lives have been touched by suicide.

It is also essential to recognize the connection between suicide, depression, and substance abuse. A high percentage of people with mood disorders and mental conditions will seek out drugs and alcohol to self medicate, which actually increases the severity of the episode and the likelihood of suicide.

Finding a treatment plan that focuses on both issues of depression/mental health disorders and substance abuse is crucial, as well as seeking out alternative therapies. Plant medicines, nutritional therapies, herbal supplements, ayurveda, yoga, meditation, exercise, bodywork, breath work, Chinese medicine, reflexology, and chiropractic just to name a few, can all be considered for your loved one, in addition to family counseling and ancestral healing modalities.

Conventional methods can sometimes be effective, but if you don't see steady progress, I'd like to encourage you to try something else! Counseling and rehab centers don't always work, and the social services programs for people who are not able to pay for the higher end facilities are often below standard. I wish I had been able to have more success with inspiring Cheyne to try alternative methods for his struggles, and I am convinced that the system he was locked into was more harmful for him than helpful.

This is a whole other conversation to unravel, and it's my hope that better services can be provided to ALL who need mental health and substance abuse support, and that sacred plant medicines and alternative modalities will be given the attention they deserve as powerful options to treat substance abuse and mental health conditions. I am very grateful for the healing support I was able to receive myself from my shamans, medicine men and women, and the plant and animal medicines that are now being medically proven to be safe and effective for many people. I see a world where these powerful natural medicines from the earth will replace harmful chemical medicines from the pharmaceutical industry.

If you are interested in learning more about this, please see the *Find Help Here* section.

It is my hope that some of this information will be useful to you, and together we can understand the hopelessness, pathology, and prevention techniques to stop the rise of suicide in our communities and across the globe.

suicide statistics

As of this writing. Please check current statistics in your community. Educating yourself about suicide and how you can help, will go a long way towards decreasing this epidemic.

- Suicide is the tenth leading cause of death among all age groups and the second leading cause of death among people aged 10-34 in the United States.
- 78% of all people who die from suicide are male.
- 50% of suicides are associated with dependency on alcohol and drugs.
- 70% of adolescent suicides are associated with alcohol and drug dependency.
- 46% of people who die from suicide had a diagnosed mental condition.
- Alcohol is a factor in 1/3 of suicides.
- Those with alcohol dependency are 10X more likely than the general public to die from suicide.
- Alcohol exacerbates the symptoms of many health conditions such as bipolar disorder, borderline personality disorder, and depression, all of which have high suicide rates.
- Mental health disorders and substance use disorders are the most significant risk factors for suicide.
- Firearms are involved in 50% of all suicides.
- Suicide is the leading cause of death for people held in local jails.
- 54% of Americans have been affected by suicide.
- 132 Americans die from suicide each day.

warning signs of suicidal ideation
. . .

Knowing the signs to look out for can help save a life!

- Increased alcohol and drug use
- Aggressive behavior
- Withdrawal from friends, family, & community
- Dramatic mood swings
- Impulsive or reckless behavior
- Collecting & saving pills or buying a weapon
- Giving away possessions
- Tying up loose ends, like organizing personal papers or paying off debts
- Saying goodbye to friends and family

Suicidal behaviors are a psychiatric emergency. If you or a loved one starts to take any of these steps, seek immediate help from a health care provide or call 911, or your local emergency line.

If you are unsure, a licensed mental health professional can help assess.

supporting a loved one experiencing suicide ideation
. . .

When a loved one is openly suicidal, or you think they could be in crisis, friends and family can often be caught off-guard, unprepared and unsure of what to do. The behaviors of a person experiencing a crisis can be unpredictable, changing dramatically without warning.

there are a few ways to approach a suicide-crisis:

1. Talk openly and be direct. Don't be afraid to ask questions like: "Are you thinking about suicide?" Saying the 'S' word acknowledges it and takes the power away.
2. Then say, 'What can I do?' or ' How can I help?' They may not have an answer, but it's worth asking and can open up the opportunity to talk about it.
3. For someone in a suicide crisis, it's ok to get specific with questions: "Do you have a plan? Do you have a method? Do you have a time frame?" *The goal is to make a connection, engage in conversation, validate feelings, and give the person a moment to feel seen and heard. Sometimes that's enough to help them begin to break out of that mind frame. Talking about suicide does not cause people to complete suicide. NOT talking about suicide might.*
4. If the person you are worried about answers "Yes", that's when you reach out to a therapist, a doctor, a family member, or trusted support. Take action and do whatever you have to do to get your loved one support!

other suggestions:

- Remove means such as guns, knives or stockpiled pills, alcohol, and drugs
- Calmly ask simple and direct questions, like "Can I help you call your psychiatrist?"
- If there are multiple people around, have one person speak at a time
- Express support and concern
- Don't argue, threaten or raise your voice
- Don't debate whether suicide is right or wrong
- If you're nervous, try not to fidget or pace
- Be patient

Whatever you do, don't keep it to yourself.

Ask for help, call one of the support organizations listed in our *Resources* section, and create a plan to support your loved one.

Do your own practices to stay calm and steady.
Pray.
Don't give up on your loved one.
Ever.
They need your love and support.

support for survivors
. . .

"She made broken look beautiful and strong look invincible.

She walked with the Universe on her shoulders and made it look like a pair of wings."

— Ariana Dancu

The pain felt by someone who has lost a loved one to suicide, called "survivors" can be harder to deal with than if the death happened by other means. The people left behind begin questioning themselves and the reasons behind suicide, wondering if they could have done something to prevent it, often take the blame themselves, and face a difficult and lonely recovery misunderstood by our society. They may be reluctant to share their stories because some people can be very insensitive.

Here are some questions and comments that were very painful for me and very common for suicide survivors to deal with:

- *How did he/she do it?*
- *Didn't you know something was wrong?*
- *He/she is in a better place now.*
- *Everyone dies at some point.*
- *At least now he/she is in a better place.*
- *Just think of all the good memories.*
- *It's in the past now, focus on the present.*
- *My dog recently died too.*

How are you?

This is probably one of the worst ones I had to face the first days, weeks, and months, after the suicide. It is well meaning, but almost impossible to answer without completely falling apart.

the *best* thing to say:

I'm so sorry. And nothing more.
You are in my thoughts/prayers. And walk away.
If you need a friend, I'm here. And then send them a message, card, or follow up.

Please take it upon yourselves to learn how to support these tender people who are facing a difficult healing journey. I know and understand this well and it is a long, lonely, and painful process.

more suggestions

1. *Be patient and compassionate.* Loss survivors grapple with complex feelings after the death of a loved one to suicide such as fear, grief, anger, and shame. Many may be dealing with the effects of trauma and PTSD after such a traumatic incident. *Accept their feelings, listen, have patience with their emotional ups and downs, and provide support WITHOUT CRITICISM OR ADVICE.*
2. *Use sensitivity around holidays, anniversaries, and birthdays,* which bring back memories of the lost loved one and emphasize their absence. Let them know you are thinking of them. *Take note that this may be for many years to come, and in some cases for the rest of their lives.*
3. *Use the lost loved one's name when talking to them.* This shows that you have not forgotten this important person in their life, and can make it easier to discuss a subject that is often stigmatized. *The loved one may not be on the planet, but they will always live in their heart.*
4. *Accept the changes in their personality and lifestyle.* Remember that the healing process of losing a loved one to suicide spans many years, and most likely a lifetime, and loss survivors may change in ways that are difficult for your relationship. Be open to allow the friendship to change so they can adapt to this life changing trauma. *They need you now more than ever, even if they seem to shut you out.*
5. *Take it upon yourself to learn how you can support them,* and don't expect them to educate you. They have enough on their plate to deal with their own healing and may not have the time or energy to gather resources for you. *Our culture does not adequately understand how to support people through grief, so doing your own research and learning how to do so is something that will have a very healing affect in creating a more compassionate and harmonious humanity.*

language matters

. . .

What we say or don't say, and how we say it, makes a difference, especially when dealing with complex life situations like suicide.

In a world where silence and insensitivity can make matters worse, learning how to use language can help create a more humane and harmonious humanity.

"Committed suicide" implies sin or crime and can cause feelings of shame and judgement to survivors of suicide.

"Died *from* suicide, or died *by* suicide," is more objective, less negative, and helps make talking about suicide easier.

A world where suicide isn't an off - limits or taboo subject can help us learn how to support each other better. When people are able to speak more openly about it, healing can happen, relationships can deepen, and more avenues of research and prevention will grow exponentially!

find help here
. . .

WithYou Forever

Your voice is dark and rich
Like the cup of coffee we share
It warms me from the inside
The smoke around us lingers
Like electric air
It was always intense with you
Just how I like it
Your bold, brown eyes
Penetrate my skin
You see the truth of me
More than I even do
Let me unmask you
Show me the way in
I know if I could just see,
I'd confirm we're the same inside
If I could do it all again
I would pick you every time
Broken hearted and all
Your soul was worth everything
Why did you hide it away?
So calm and cool
Firm and gentle, together
You didn't get to see me at my best
I should have been better for you
I think you would be happy now
If you could have held on with me, Cheyne
We made it to the lifeboat

~Adrienne DeWitt

UNITED STATES:

The 988 Suicide & Crisis Lifeline/ The National Suicide Prevention Lifeline

A national network of local crisis centers that provides free and confidential emotional support to people in suicidal crisis or emotional distress 24 hours a day, 7 days a week in the United States. They are committed to improving crisis services and advancing suicide prevention by empowering individuals, advancing professional best practices, and building awareness.

988.lifeline.org
800-273-TALK (8255)

BeFrienders Worldwide

Members and volunteers around the world provide confidential emotional support to people when they are suicidal. The centers also alleviate misery, loneliness, despair and depression by listening to anyone who feels they have nowhere else to turn. The people who run the centers - befrienders - are volunteers who have all been specially trained. The work is non-political and non-religious, and volunteers do not try to impose their convictions on anyone. They simply listen. The fact that someone has been in contact with a center - whether by telephone, letter, email or in a face-to-face meeting - is strictly confidential.

befrienders.org

HELPLINE

Free emotional support, anywhere, anytime in United States, India, and Canada.

Helplines (also known as hotlines or crisis lines) provide immediate crisis counseling, emotional support and information – for free. Most helpline phone numbers are toll-free and many helplines are available over text message or online chat. Helplines are often available 24/7, so you can contact them at any time of the day or night.

FINDAHELPLINE.COM

Monica Mesa Dasi & Cheyne Mesa-Salley

INTERNATIONAL ASSOCIATION FOR SUICIDE PREVENTION

The International Association for Suicide Prevention is dedicated to preventing suicide and suicidal behavior and alleviating its effects. IASP leads the global role in suicide prevention by strategically developing an effective forum that is proactive in creating strong collaborative partnerships and promoting evidence-based action in order to reduce the incidence of suicide and suicidal behavior.
The World Health Organization (WHO) estimates more than 700,000 people die due to suicide each year and that almost 77% of all global suicides occur in low and middle-income communities/countries. For every suicide there are many more who attempt suicide or have serious suicidal ideation. Suicidal behavior profoundly impacts families and communities and remains a universal challenge with millions impacted. The reduction of suicide mortality is of global importance and a vital public health consideration.

IASP.INFO

Support in Crested Butte, Colorado:

Crested Butte State of Mind

CB State of Mind (CBSOM) is a grassroots organization created by the community to reduce the high rate of suicide in the valley. Their work is based on the foundation and belief that suicide is preventable and everyone can play a role in preventing it. Through decreasing stigma, increasing support/education, and increasing access, they aim to save lives.

Suicide is the 7th leading cause of death in Gunnison County, where access to mental health providers is lower than in many other parts of the state. In addition, the severity of substance abuse issues in the community has become so significant that mental health, with contributing factors such as alcohol and drug abuse, is a major priority in the county. The mission of CB State of Mind is to connect the community to resources, education, and free counseling scholarships to improve mental wellness, eliminate stigma, and lower the rate of suicide in the Gunnison Valley.

CB State of Mind is committed to making sure that residents of the community have access to mental health care, and that means eliminating the barriers of cost, navigating the system, and connecting to the right service. Scholarships are available for up to 10 sessions if locating and paying for therapy is a challenge for local residents. Volunteer opportunities and donations are available in any amount. There is no contribution too small to make a big impact that provides immediate mental health support to community members who are in need, and to abate the suicide concerns in the community. You can also make your donation *in Cheyne's honor* by including his name on the online application.

CBSTATEOFMIND.ORG

HELPFUL BOOKS

There are so many wonderful resources available depending on your individual circumstances, and these are some books that have been so supportive to me on the healing journey.

No Death, No Fear: Comforting Wisdom for Life
~Thich Nhat Hanh

It's Ok That You're Not OK
~Megan Devine

The Smell of Rain on Dust
~Martin Prechtel

Becoming Supernatural: How Common People Are Doing the Uncommon
~Dr. Joe Dispenza

When Things Fall Apart: Heart Advice for Difficult Times
~Pema Chodron

What the New science of Psychedelics Teaches Us About Consciousness, Dying, Addiction, Depression, & Transcendence
~Michael Pollan

The Book of Joy
~His Holiness the Dalai Lama & Archbishop Desmond Tutu

Atlas of the Heart
~Brene' Brown

The Bhagavad Gita
~Translated by Eknath Easwaran

soulful acknowledgements

Photo by Cheyne. Crested Butte, CO

From Cheyne:

I'd like to honor all those who loved me, tried to help me, and brought so much joy to my life. Especially my mother and father, Monica Mesa Dasi and Hiver Salley, who gave me life. My brothers, Skye and Ronin, who gave me a reason to live, and brought me so much joy, brotherhood, and unforgettable memories. To the Crested Butte community, and the majesty of the mountains that held me up and gave me epic adventures and inspiration. I lived and breathed for you, and I hope you'll find something in this book, even one thing, that you can grab onto and live your life to the fullest. Endless gratitude to my mom, having the courage to write this book and get my messages out there into the hands of those who need it, for getting her will to live back, and open her heart to continue our relationship in the formless reality.

I'm smiling from heaven and sending love to you all.

From Monica:

My heart is exploding in gratitude for all these people and forces that helped me survive the tragedy of my lifetime:

For **Cheyne**, my sun, my Guru, my first son, who gave me the gift of motherhood and chose me to be his karma companion in this life and beyond. You expanded my heart and gave me a *soul on fire* to know the depths of love and a passion to teach people the power of self love, and the sacred mission to be a beneficial presence on the planet. Infinite gratitude for the 25 years of loving you and the extraordinary lesson that a soul never dies. Thank you for keeping our relationship alive and for all the messages you have sent me! You are withMe forever.

For **Skye and Ronin**, my other two sons, who gave Cheyne the gift of brotherhood, have shown me the way of a warrior, the sacred masculine, and have stood by my side through it all. You are my number one reason to keep living this life with purpose and joy.

For the **God** of my understanding, the Universal Power that is all-knowing, all-powerful, and ever-present in my life. This mysterious power that I am One with gives me strength, hope and courage to heal my soul, my lineage, and be a force of change in the world.

For my mother, **Irma Mesa**, who gave me life, love, has always been my number one believer, and whose unconditional love has rescued me and shown me the power of a mother's love.

For my father, **Hugo Mesa**, who also made my life possible, taught me to always be myself, understood Cheyne in a way many couldn't, and has shown me the way of forgiveness and a father's love that every daughter needs.

For **Jackie Just**, my editor, you started off as a humble work-trade staff at Yoga For The Peaceful, quickly became the best manager and teacher I've ever trained, then went on to become my business partner in my online programs. You are a friend, student, daughter of my heart, and now one of my own teachers and coaches and the best heartful editor I could have ever dreamed of. Thank you for typing, and crying with me, as I read out Cheyne's words, held space while I relived the grief, and believed in me and this book. Without you, so much of my life, including this book, would simply not have happened, and certainly not with so much joy and transformation. My karmic sister, I love you. I believe in you. I'm endlessly grateful to you and I know we have many more adventures to share!

For my sister **Lucy**, who ran to my side like a firefighter in a wild fire, and spoiled, adored, and showered Cheyne with her special auntie love.

For my sister **Corinne**, who came to us later in life with only joy, sparkles, and a Grace that has been one of the greatest blessings in our family, and to her mother, **Valerie**, who gifted her to us and loved my beloved father just the way he needed, and has always been an anchor for us all.

For **Shiva Rea**, who gave me many life-saving practices of yoga, is a living embodiment of the Goddess, and showed up for me instantly and powerfully.

For **Lama Tsultrim Allione**, my Lama in the Tantric Buddhist path, who came swiftly to my side, and all the teachers and practices I have learned that support me to this day.

For **KT Joy Folz**, our "family shaman", who was a warrior angel that created a forcefield around me in the first few days that quite possibly saved my life, and created a memorial service for Cheyne in our Crested Butte community that was a healing nectar for us all. Her blend of wisdom and heart fire has been steadfast for my sons and I.

For **Betsy Cohen**, the friend that only comes once in a lifetime, who received every hysterical call, cry for help, and never to this day stops living my grief journey along side me. Cheyne's "other mother" in childhood, she knew him as a wee-one, gave him his best friend in her son Elias Friedman, and continues to show me the way of the wise woman and everlasting friendship.

For **Mark Dodds**, thank you for being with me through the toughest years of Cheyne's life, for rescuing him so many times, and for making him, and all of us, laugh and get through those hard times.

For **Karie Reyes**, another angel on her own grief journey, who created images for me throughout the years, including many images of Cheyne that brought me to my knees, including some of the images and poems in this book. Thank you for your love, support, sisterhood, friendship, and your belief and faith in me. Your images created from your heart, poems you've shared with me, and strength and wisdom have been a true gift.

For **Emily Croharé**, so much more than my "assistant" who also shares a grief journey, is one of the most talented teachers I've ever had the pleasure to come through my teacher training, and whose deep love and friendship has been the anchor for my business. You were responsible for making all of my offerings possible, you capture my true spirit, do everything with polish and grit, might drive me crazy sometimes, but damn, you make it fun!

For **Meghan Neeley**, my business coach who showed me the way to continue to create offerings that enabled me to continue to support myself through the grief process.

For **Laurie Tessler**, and all my beloved friends and family all over the world, who held me up and supported me in so many miraculous ways.

For **Aaron Fisher,** author of Love Letters, who inspired me to write this book, and believed in me all the way through!

For **Monique Alvarez,** my publisher who believed in this heart project, supported me with her compassion and passion, and created the beautiful book you are now holding.

For **Kory Lon Tydon**, for believing in my dream of authoring books and gave me the sacred pause I needed to make it a reality. Cheyne brought you to me, you brought me back to Cheyne's reincarnation, and we are forever karmically bonded.

For my Gurus: Neem Karoli Baba, and Mata Amritanandamayi / Amma, who opened my heart of devotion and Bhakti Yoga, the path of love, service and devotion.

For all my healers, counselors, therapists, plant medicine shamans, and mystics, who continue to support me on my healing journey; Jean Bell Dumas, Marcie Telander, Andi Tippie, Dana Hersh, Judi Theis, Taita Juanito, Don Florentino, Mama Jairzagua, David Tayar, Oscar Ramírez, and more.

For the **Crested Butte Community**, an endless list of people who saw our family through all its trials and tribulations, gave Cheyne the best home, friends, work, mountains and streams to play in, and provided a support system for my family that will never be forgotten. My home for over 25 years, the place of Cheyne's gravesite, it will always be my hOMe and where I will one day rest along side him.

For **Yoga For The Peaceful**, the studio that I created with the support of my angel, **Juliet Stillman**. Through her partnership and faith in me, I was able to create a healing sanctuary for our community, all who visited, and a place that I could carry out my mission to bring the practices of my heart to all. Yoga For The Peaceful was there for me while I raised Cheyne, Skye, and Ronin through all the challenges, and held me up with an outpouring of love and support.

For **all my students**, mentees, and people I coached in my Soul on Fire online annual programs. They accepted, loved me, and gave me the great joy and honor to continue my work while I was going through the harrowing process of recovery from Cheyne's passing. They gave me purpose, and inspired me to continue serving my gifts and heal while I helped others heal.

For **all the people** who sent letters, food, text messages, gifts, money, social media comments and messages, prayers, and an endless list of support, many of which I may never be able to thank personally. Your selfless and generous support was an extraordinary blessing that can only be repaid by God's grace.

I am forever grateful!

For **Mother Earth**'s mountain majesty, endless waves, nordic trails, rivers and streams, butterflies and flowers, oh, how I love you. I bow to you in deep gratitude for holding me, and surrounding me with God's miraculous beauty and inspiration.

For the one who's holding my heart now, may it be forever.

For **all of you** reading this far, it's because of you that this oracle of love, that Cheyne wanted me to share with you, is now my living legacy.

Thank you ALL, from my deepest soul on fire!

about the author

Monica Mesa Dasi is a Tantrik yogini, intuitive, writer, mother of three sons, and devotee of beloved Gurus Neem Karoli Baba and Amma. She is a deeply trusted mentor, channeler, plant medicine woman, and an activist that leads the *Soul on Fire* Movement.

Monica has impacted the physical, mental and spiritual lives of people around the globe with her message of self-love, the power of daily practice, and the importance to fearlessly claim your mission and be a beneficial presence on the planet. She is a presenter at festivals, retreats, global events, and teaches inspiring online courses.

Monica's spiritual path and practices have inspired her to launch transformational programs that focus on the *"Three Gems of Healing"*: self love, the power of practice, and purpose-based living. These three gems form the foundation of all her *Soul on Fire* programs. Her message, **"love yourself and you love the world"** is what she believes will give rise to personal and planetary healing for a more compassionate, healthy, and harmonious humanity.

Monica can be found living in the mountains and by the sea, surfing, serving, loving, devoted to her daily practices, being a proud mama to her sons, and endlessly believing in a world where all beings can be happy and free.

www.monicamesadasi.com
FB/IG @monicamesadasi

The Four Immeasurables

May all beings have happiness
And the causes of happiness.

May all beings be free from suffering
And the causes of suffering.

May all beings never be separate from the supreme JOY
That is beyond sorrow.

May all beings abide in equanimity
Free from attachment and aversion.

photo credit: Andi Tippie

a parting song

See my hands and look at my feet
It's OK if it's hard to believe
I have faith you will do greater things
It's my time to go, but before I leave

Go tell the world about me!

I was dead, but now I live
I've gotta go now for a little while
But goodbye is not the end

Don't forget the things that I taught you
I've conquered death, and I hold the keys
Where I go, you will go to, someday
But there's much to do here before you leave

A Parting Song

Go tell the world about me!

I was dead, but now I live
I've gotta go now for a little while
But goodbye is not the end of the journey, the end of
    the road

My spirit is with you wherever you go
You have a purpose and I have a plan
I will make you this promise
I'll come back again but until then

Go tell the world about me!

I was dead, but now I live
I've gotta go now for a little while
But goodbye is not the end

Go tell them about me!
Go tell the world
Go tell the world
I've got to go for a little while
But goodbye is not the end

The Commission
~Song by Cain

Made in United States
Troutdale, OR
08/14/2023

12070825R00166